Manipulat Dark Psychology

A Complete Guide to Excel in the Art of Persuasion, improving your Social Skills for Leadership, Influencing People and Increasing your Emotional Intelligence

© **Copyright 2021 - All rights reserved.**

The content contained within this book may not be reproduced, duplicated, or transmitted without direct written permission from the author or the publisher.

Under no circumstances will any blame or legal responsibility be held against the publisher, or author, for any damages, reparation, or monetary loss due to the information contained within this book. Either directly or indirectly.

Legal Notice:

This book is copyright protected. This book is only for personal use. You cannot amend, distribute, sell, use, quote or paraphrase any part, or the content within this book, without the consent of the author or publisher.

Disclaimer Notice:

Please note the information contained within this document is for educational and entertainment purposes only. All effort has been executed to present accurate, up to date, and reliable, complete information. No warranties of any kind are declared or implied. Readers acknowledge that the author is not engaging in the rendering of legal, financial, medical, or professional advice. The content within this book has been derived from various sources.

Please consult a licensed professional before attempting any techniques outlined in this book.

By reading this document, the reader agrees that under no circumstances is the author responsible for any losses, direct or indirect, which are incurred as a result of the use of the information contained within this document, including, but not limited to, — errors, omissions, or inaccuracies.

Table of Contents

Introduction 9
   How Manipulation Works 9
Chapter 1 Effective Communication and How to Enhance Your Social Skills 15
   Importance of Communication Skills 15
   Point to Note 15
   Non-Verbal Communication 16
   Conversation Skills 17
   Assertiveness 17
   Persuasion and Influencing Skills 18
   Communication Skills 18
   Conflict Management Skills 19
   Leadership Skills 19
   Change Management Skills 20
   Building Rapport 20
   Team-Working 21
Chapter 2 Techniques for Effective Communication 23
   Neuro-Linguistic Programming (NLP) 23
   Self-Hypnosis 26
Chapter 3 Leadership 29
   Leaders Are Not Followers 29
   Carries the Vision That Will Inspire Others 30
   A Great Leader Is A Coach 30
   Value Effectiveness, Not Efficiency 31
   Adapt to Change Easily 31
   Great Leaders Are Effective Listeners 32
   Accepts Responsibility 33

Builds Relationships 33
Leaders Celebrate 33
Chapter 4 Manipulations in Dark Psychology 35

1. Lying 36
2. Rotating the Truth 36
3. Withdrawal of Affection.. 36
4. Sarcastic Jokes 37
5. Make Subject Feel Helpless 37
6. Use of Aggression 37
7. Plays the Role of Victim 38
8. Pretending Ignorance... 38
9. Threats.. 38
10. Emotional Blackmailing 39
11. Pretending Empathy... 39
12. Positive Reinforcement.. 39
13. Minimization... 40

Chapter 5 How to Make Friends and Influence Others 41

Fine Tuning 42
Setting a Rapport Using Tuning... 44
Adjustment to Physiology 45
Partial Adjustment.. 46
Macro Fine Tuning.. 48
Micro Fine Tuning... 50
Adjustment to the Voice 51

Chapter 6 How to Persuade Some One of Your Opinion............ 53

Let the Structure of Your Request Be in Optimal Order 53
Give Them A Chance to Speak.. 55
Match Their Reasoning 55
Present Your Counterargument 56

Adjust the Speed of Your Speech to The Audiences 57
Chapter 7 How to Put Your Views Across to Someone in Authority
....59

   Communicating Your Views and Needs Effectively 61
Chapter 8 Influence People With Principles of Persuasion 66

   Reciprocity..66
   Consistency 67
   Social Validation..68
   Liking...69
   Scarcity 70
   Authority 70
Chapter 9 Emotional Intelligence 71

   What is Emotional Intelligence? 72
   Traits of High Emotional Intelligence 7
   The Four Emotional Intelligence Domains 77
   How Emotional Intelligence Influences Others....................81
Chapter 10 Dark Manipulation Techniques 86

Chapter 11 Developing Mind Control...96

   Mind Control 96
   Who Uses Mind Control?..99
Chapter 12 How to Analyze People Using Dark Psychology 10

   Word Choice 10
   Body Language 107
   Behavior 108
   Vibes..110
   Appearance 110
Chapter 13 Tactics to Manipulate Others 114

   Techniques of Manipulation 117
   Apply Different Persuasion and Manipulation 122

Techniques 122
Chapter 14 How to Understand and Connect With Other People's Emotions 125
   Social - Being Liked 129
   Authority... 129
   Consistency 130
   Storytelling... 131
   Paradoxical Intervention 132
   Examples of Reverse Psychology 132
Chapter 15 Deception 133
   Starting Your Deception.. 135
   Tell Your Own Story 136
   Tips for Lying Effectively 138
Conclusion 142

Introduction

Manipulation is a form of social influence that uses indirect, underhanded, and deceptive tactics to change people's perceptions and resulting behavior. Usually, the end goal is to advance the interests of the person who initiates the manipulation. In many cases, manipulation happens at the expense of the person being manipulated; who may end up emotionally, mentally, or physically harmed, or taking actions against their own best interests.

It's important to note that social influence is not inherently bad; one person can use manipulation techniques for the good of the person they are manipulating. For example, your family members or friends can use social influence and manipulation to get you to do something for your good. The people who mean you well might manipulate you as a way to help you deal with certain challenges or to make you choose the right decisions.

How Manipulation Works

Several psychological theories explain how successful manipulation works. The first theory, and perhaps the most universally accepted, is the one proposed by the famous psychologist and writer George Simon. He analyzed the concept of manipulation from the point of view of the manipulator, and he came up with a pattern of behavior that sums up every manipulation scenario. According to Simon, three main elements are involved in psychological manipulation.

First, the manipulator approaches the target by concealing his or her aggressive intentions. Here, the manipulator seeks to endear himself to his target without revealing the fact that his ultimate plan is to manipulate him or her. The manipulator accomplishes this by modifying his behavior and presenting himself as a goodnatured and friendly individual who relates well with the target.

Secondly, the manipulator will take time to know the victim. The purpose of this is to understand the psychological vulnerabilities that the victim may have to figure out which manipulation tactic will be the most effective when he ultimately decides to deploy them.

Depending on the scenario, and the complexity of the manipulation technique, this stage may take anywhere between a few minutes to several years. For example, when a stranger targets you, he may take only a couple of minutes to "size you up," but when your partner or colleague seeks to manipulate you, he or she may spend months or even years trying to understand how your mind works.

The success of this second step depends on how well the first step is executed. If the manipulator successfully hides his intentions from you, he is in a better position to learn your weaknesses because you will instill some level of trust in him, and he will use that trust to get you to let down your guard and to reveal your vulnerabilities to him.

Thirdly, having collected enough information to act upon, the manipulator will deploy a manipulation technique of his choosing. For this to work, the manipulator needs to marshal a sufficient level of ruthlessness; this means that the manipulation technique chosen will depend on what the manipulator can tolerate. A manipulator with a conscience may try to use methods that are less harmful to manipulate you. One that completely lacks a conscience may use extreme methods to take advantage of you. Either way, manipulative people are willing to let harm befall their victims, and to them, the outcome (which is usually in their favor) justifies the harm they cause.

Simon's manipulation theory teaches us the general approach that manipulators use to get what they want from their victims. Still, it also points out something extremely important: Manipulation works, not just because of the manipulator's actions, but also because of the reactions of the victims. If we were to look back at the three stages of manipulation that we have discussed, you would notice that the manipulation can fail at any of the steps if the victim catches on the manipulator's intentions.

In the first step, the manipulator misrepresents himself to the victim: If the victim can see through the veil that the manipulator is wearing, the manipulation won't be successful. In the second step, the manipulator collects information about victims to learn about his or her vulnerabilities. The victim can be able to stop the manipulation at this stage by treating the manipulator's prying nature with a bit of suspicion. In the third stage, the manipulator uses coercive or underhanded techniques to get what he wants from the victim. Even in this stage, the victim may have certain choices on how to react to the manipulator's machinations.

The point here is that when it comes to manipulation, it takes two to tango. By understanding both the victim's and the manipulator's psychology, it's possible to figure out how you can avoid falling victim to other people's manipulation, and it can also help you become more conscientious so that you don't unknowingly use manipulation techniques on other people around you.

Let's look at the vulnerabilities that manipulators like to exploit in their victims.

The first and most prevalent vulnerability is the need to please others. We all have this need to some extent; we seek to please the people in our lives and total strangers. This is technically a positive quality that helps us coexist in our societies, but it is a weapon that can be used against you by manipulators. Many of us are willing to endure certain levels of discomfort just to make other people feel happy; we feel a certain sense of obligation towards one another, and that's just human nature. The closer we are to certain people, the greater the need to please them. For example, the need to please your friend is higher than your need to please a stranger.
Manipulators understand this, and they use it against their victims all the time. If a manipulator wants to get something big out of you, he will first take the time to get closer to you, not just to get to know your vulnerability, but also to increase the sense of obligation you feel towards him. The second vulnerability is the need for approval and acceptance. Again, as social beings, we all have an innate desire to feel accepted. We want people to love us, think of us as members of their groups, and choose us over other people. This feeling can be addictive, and it can give other people (especially manipulative ones) a lot of power over us. The vast majority of manipulation victims are people who have close personal relationships with the manipulators; in other words, they have an emotional need to gain the acceptance or approval of the manipulator. The remaining manipulation victims can be manipulated because they want to be a part of something (a group, a social class, etc.).
The third vulnerability that manipulators like to exploit is what psychologists refer to as "emetophobia" (which is the fear of negative emotions). To some extent, we are all afraid of negative emotions; we will do lots of things to avoid feeling angry, afraid, stressed, frustrated, and worried, etc. We want

to lead happy and fulfilled lives, and anything that makes us feel "bad" is a threat to that sense of fulfillment. So, in many cases, we will do what manipulators want if it serves to alleviate that "bad" feeling. Manipulators know this, and they use negative emotions against us all the time.

The fourth vulnerability is the lack of assertiveness.

Assertiveness is a very rare quality; even people who you may generally consider to be assertive are likely to cave in if manipulators push hard enough. Even when you are willing to stand your ground and to say "No," manipulators can be very persistent, and in the end, they can wear you out.

The fifth vulnerability is the lack of a strong sense of identity. Having a strong sense of identity means having clear personal boundaries and understanding one's values. Unfortunately, these qualities aren't so strong in most of us, leaving us open to manipulation. Manipulators succeed by pushing our boundaries little by little, making them blurry, and then taking control of our identities.

Finally, having an external locus of control and having a low level of self-reliance are also key vulnerabilities that manipulators love to exploit. When you have an external locus of control, it means that your identity and your sense of self are external to you. It means you view yourself through other people's eyes. It means that you are extrinsically motivated. When you have low self-reliance, it means you depend on other people for sustenance and emotional stability. It means that if support systems in your life are taken away, you can easily find yourself leaning on a manipulator, which leaves you at his mercy.

Chapter 1 Effective Communication and How to Enhance Your Social Skills

Importance of Communication Skills

They are the most important skills that can help you develop and keep friendships and build crucial social networks. Communication skills can also help you take care of your needs while at the same time being appreciative of the needs of other people. It is common knowledge that no one is born with good communication skills, but like all other skills, you can learn them through trial and error by practicing daily. Areas of communication that you have to practice regularly include:

- Conversation skills

- Assertiveness

- Non-verbal communication

Point to Note

There are many aspects to effective communication, and you may want more help in specified areas such as providing feedback, dealing with conflicts, and learning how to present.

Non-Verbal Communication

A large part of what people communicate to each other nonverbally. What you say to people with your body language or eyes is as important as what you utter. However, your tone of voice and body language does communicate messages to other people regarding your:

- Honesty (do you have any secret intention?)

- Attitude towards the listener (for example, contempt and submissiveness)

- Knowledge of the subject

- Emotional state or condition (for example, fear and impatience)

Therefore, if you are used to standing far away from other people, deliberately avoiding eye contact, and speaking quietly, you are simply saying, "Please stay away from me!" or "Please do not speak to me!" Sometimes, the chances may be that this is not the message that you wish to pass across.

Conversation Skills

One of the most challenging things to do if you have social anxiety is initiating a conversation and keeping it going. It is normal to struggle a bit when trying to start a talk because it is not easy to think of the things to say. This is usually the case, especially when you are anxious. Besides, some anxious people speak too much, which may negatively impact other people.

Assertiveness

Assertive communication is the expression of your feelings, wants, and needs honestly while making sure that you respect those of other people. When you express your thoughts assertively, you prove that you are non-judgmental and nonthreatening, and you are responsible for your actions. Social skills concern the skills required to manage and impact the emotions of other people effectively. Even though this sounds like manipulation, it essentially initiates a positive emotion and gets others to positively manifest their emotions. In this way, emotional skills can be regarded as the ultimate piece of the emotional jigsaw. A revisit of emotional intelligence indicates that it begins with understanding your emotions, which is self-awareness competence. Once you have understood your emotions, the next step is to handle them in what is known as self-regulation. With managed emotions, you can use them to accomplish your goals in what is known as self-motivation. If you understand and handle yourself, you will begin to comprehend others' feelings in what is regarded as empathy, and eventually, you will influence them in what is regarded as social skills.

In this manner, social skills will include the ability to persuade and impact skills in others. Social skills will also include communication skills and conflict management skills. If you possess social skills concerning emotional intelligence, then you will also possess leadership skills. Change management skills are part of social skills, and building rapport is another social skill applied in emotional intelligence. One must also possess collaboration and cooperation competencies to become socially skilled within the context of emotional intelligence. Against this backdrop, the following is a detailed discussion of requisite competencies to build your social skills within the context of emotional intelligence.

Persuasion and Influencing Skills

The art of enticing others and convincing them to absorb your ideas is known as persuasion. People who are persuasive or have an impact will read the emotional currents in a situation and perfect what they are saying to appeal to the spur involved. Persuasion is a function of communication and personality, and this demands that you become an effective communicator who is empathetic to others. Winning over people involves trying to convince them to join your course. You must learn to sell your views as a salesperson would do.

Communication Skills

Good emotional intelligence requires good communication skills. Learn to listen to others and channel your thoughts and your feelings. Make the people around you understand what it is you are communicating and look for the full and open sharing of information. Part of communication skills will require that you become prepared to learn about challenges and not just want to receive good news. If you are a good communicator, you will handle challenging issues directly as opposed to letting problems compile. Ensure that the message you are packaging is appropriate and then register and act on emotional cues when communicating.

Conflict Management Skills

Conflicts are unavoidable and sometimes not predictable. Both at home and work, the art of handling and resolving conflict is important. Conflict management skills begin with becoming aware of critical tact and diplomacy and how these competencies can be applied to defuse emotive situations. If you are a good conflict manager, you will manage to expose disagreements and help resolve them. Most importantly, conflict resolution does not involve you dictating the solution; it is rather helping the affected parties identify the different opinions, fears, and shared understanding to craft a solution. The competence of conflict resolution entails deploying sharing of emotions to motivate debate and open discussion and lessening the underlying problems. When resolving conflict, more emphasis should be placed on the logical position, as this is often the shared understanding among the conflicting parties.

Leadership Skills

Emotional intelligence and leadership skills are connected in multiple ways. The ability to influence requires that you tune your emotions and those of others to win them over. Influence is a critical attribute of good leadership. It is sometimes called charisma, but leadership skills involving influence go beyond charisma to match good emotional intelligence. The competencies of good leadership require you to articulate a vision and those other people with it. You do not have to be in a formal leadership position to give leadership. While holding your colleagues accountable, support and direct their performance. Learn to lead by example.

Change Management Skills

Change catalysts can be effective managers, individuals that make positive change while involving everyone. For all people involved, change tends to create pressure, partly because of the fear of the unknown. Good change management requires to turn change into an exciting opportunity rather than a threat. Change catalysts recognize the importance of change and remove barriers. Change catalysts disrupt the status quo and advocate for transformation. Leading by example is a common attribute of change catalysts to trigger desired adjustments.

Building Rapport

It is important to create and maintain constructive relationships with other people. Mastering this skill will lead to improved relationships and increased ability to work and succeed in life. People who are good with building bonds are great networkers, create and sustain a robust network of connections and contacts. Creating a rapport involves establishing relationships to keep it healthy. If you exhibit good rapport as a competence, then you are likely to have many friends. The essence of bonding is valuing others and taking an interest in their lives and being eager to learn more about them.

Team-Working

People with good collaboration skills will build good and useful productive working and other relationships, and some people function well with others. All these attributes are vital when building social skills in emotional intelligence. People with collaborative skills will see relationships as critical as the pending task and will value people as much as they consider the activity at hand. If you have collaboration skills, you will actively cooperate, share ideas and plans, and work with others to create an improved product. The best environment will attract other people to contribute. If you possess the competency of collaboration and cooperation, you will actively seek opportunities for cooperative work. A team will perform better when good team-workers are present in the group and this tends to attract other members to join the team. Good team-workers help the team build an identity and foster commitment.

Chapter 2 Techniques for Effective Communication

You are at an advantage when you can communicate effectively. After all, you are the person who knows your goals and how you hope to achieve them. The point is that you are not going to achieve those goals single-handedly, because you don't live in isolation. Every single one of us needs allies, friends, and supporters along the way. How do you work with other people unless you can get your point across? How can you develop strong and lasting allegiances unless you understand what's going on with the people you work with? Earlier, we discussed building influence and how you can achieve that through a variety of strategic devices and being someone who models excellence in all you do. Now we'll look at some other techniques to support what we've already learned.

Following are some useful psychological techniques that help in effective communication:

Neuro-Linguistic Programming (NLP)

Created in the 1970s by two California doctors (Drs. Bandler and

Grinder), neuro-linguistic programming employs theories of psychoanalysis and communication to help people develop themselves more fully. NLP advances the idea that many of our behaviors are programmed and can be altered for the better because of a link through linguistic and neurological realities. There are strong links between what we do, what we say and how we behave that Drs. Bandler and Grinder believed, in developing NLP, could be useful in modifying undesirable or socially unviable behaviors. Moreover, they believed that these alterations would lead to dramatic improvements in the quality of relationships and professional lives of those who used these techniques.

NLP's goal is to understand how the human mind perceives things; how to use all your senses comprehensively to effectively send your intended message through verbal and non-verbal communication. NLP can also help you apply this understanding to communicate more effectively by creating rapport between you and other people. Needless to say, how you present yourself and what you have to say matters a lot regarding the way others perceive you. When our neurolinguistic patterning provokes behaviors that prevent effective communication, this can be "repatterned" to deliver better results.

Does it mean you are failing if you can't persuade someone to change their mind or budge on a dearly held position?

The answer is no. It just means you need a bit of personal tweaking. As we've discussed throughout this book, part of that has to do with understanding yourself and how you present to others. It also has to do with applying that knowledge to your perceptions about other people. But when it comes to our behaviors (some of which have to do with nonverbal language), perhaps NLP is the silver bullet to more successful and fruitful interactions with other people. With your sharpened communication skills, you will still be fostering a constructive work environment, because NLP helps do that by the following characteristics:

- Helps you communicate clearly.

- Helps you have a positive personal impact on people.

- Helps you build trust among colleagues and friends.

- Helps you put people at ease and, by doing so, elicit sincere reactions and feedback from them.

- Helps you build respect among colleagues and friends.

- Helps you appreciate other people's point of view, even when it differs from your own.

- Helps you use the existing climate to bring about your preferred outcome.

And what is the result of using the NLP technique?

- Your workplace team can reiterate what you have communicated to them correctly and mirror your intentions, ensuring they deliver the desired outcomes.

- You provide your team with the opportunity to express their opinions, even when they differ from your own. This tension is healthy and encourages creative dissent, which can build the team through confidence in your leadership and the validity of team opinions.

- Your technique can enhance the impact of your verbal message, serving a complementary role. For example, a pat on the back, delivered in concert with a verbal message of approval for a job well done, has a reinforcing effect, which complements the spoken message.

- You can underline your verbal message when you throw your hands in the air as you verbalize your exasperation. That is called "accenting".

All of these changes in your communications style are possible with NLP. Of course, seeking out a trained professional to assist you with the process is highly recommended. If you feel that resorting to clinical help is necessary to help you succeed in life in places where you have gotten "stuck", it's well worth considering.

Self-Hypnosis

Just for clarification, this technique has nothing to do with the "Svengali effect", in which a stage hypnotist attempts to overwhelm your autonomy, inducing you to submit to his charismatic control. Life is not a movie. Here you are not going to learn how to put anyone in a trance. This technique is concerned with fostering effective communication by encouraging your mind to work at a higher level. You will learn to clear out distracting thoughts from your environment and delve deeply into your thought processes. By following this technique, you can understand what you want and how you intend to go about getting it. You will also learn to decipher non-verbal cues you have noted in your interactions with others, providing you with an objective reading of all

factors in any given situation. This process can enhance your objectivity and improve your ability to make rationally-informed and sound decisions.
In short, self-hypnosis helps you achieve the following:

- Avoid distractions and improve concentration.

- Solve problems by having a better and more wellrounded understanding of them.

- Formulate ideas as part of a strategic plan you can then put into practice.

Taking the time to train your mind to be quiet and to make space for rapid analysis and evaluation is a worthwhile pursuit. It may sound a little unorthodox, but making it possible for your brain to make decisions based on careful analysis, instead of being alive with detritus that's not serving you in the project of moving forward with your life, is something that can genuinely make you more effective in every area of your life. Self-hypnosis can help you achieve this.

Chapter 3 Leadership

You have heard it said that employees do not leave companies; they leave bad managers. Well, this is true because if you asked around, one in two employees fled from a lousy manager. As a leader, these statistics should concern you. Looking at the statement above carefully, the employees do not flee from leaders; they run away from managers. This means that there is a significant difference between a leader and a manager. However, managers can learn and adopt leadership behaviors and build a team that is resilient, accountable, proactive, trustworthy, and passionate, dedicated to their work and the accomplishment of the company mission.

To become a good leader, here are some behaviors you ought to develop so that you can positively impact your team's dedication and productivity.

Leaders Are Not Followers

Leaders aim to set the pace, not follow others. If you come across a company that lacks innovation, one that is always following and copying what other companies are doing, be confident that it is always lagging in terms of progress and development.

A leader best learns from experience and from mentors who have gone before them. A leader is also a servant to the stakeholders. However, there is a difference between learning, serving, and following. A good leader will serve others and learn from others' experiences, but will aim to carve out his path. He will have a unique, innovative way of doing things, and when it comes to decision-making, the leader will trust his gut or intuition rather than follow in the steps other leaders are taking.

Carries the Vision That Will Inspire Others

Leaders are vision-bearers. He comes up with a concept and sells it to others, who then follow it if they deem it fit. A leader influences others to act, relying on the vision of their leader, hoping that it will get them to the expected end.

A Great Leader Is A Coach

Experts and the results from various studies conducted in the corporate sector say that companies can only achieve the best development results when the employees and the leaders are actively engaged in the processes. Taking a coaching approach to leadership makes it easier for the leader to develop a partnership relationship with his juniors, and from there they can build a shared vision for what they need to do to accomplish the set goals.

Coaching gives the leader an active and more personal take in everyone's personal and career development in his team. Through close interaction, the leader can also discover his employees' personal needs, unique circumstances, personal goals, and the challenges they face. From there, he can tune his company's employee appraisal policies to be aligned with the employees' needs.

If you have watched episodes from the show 'The Undercover Boss,' you have seen how bosses disguise themselves and go to various company locations to interact with their employees and see how operations are running. The result is often that the bosses get a chance to interact with their employees oneon-one and end up discovering the unique challenges they are facing, either at work or in their personal lives. The bosses then help them out or iron out policies so that the employees no longer experience the same challenges. This is how the relationship between employees and their bosses ought to be all year round.

Value Effectiveness, Not Efficiency

It is not in a leader's job description to worry about productivity, efficiency, optimization, and fine-tuning; that is the manager's work. Instead, a leader is concerned about the dream or the vision and how to get there. However, there will be unique incidences where a leader also functions as the manager, and he will take on the managerial roles, such as ensuring that there is continuous improvement of the quality of the product.

Adapt to Change Easily

A great leader will quickly change focus when the situation demands it, such as when the needs of the organization change. Adaptable people surround themselves with equally minded people, and in an organization, this mentality creates a culture of learning and taking risks, which is a precursor for growth and innovation in the company.

Adaptable leaders tend to operate at their peak because they have made their work enjoyable. It is no longer a bundle of routine tasks, but the chance to work through a series of exciting events and new circumstances. As such, the leaders continually push themselves and their employees to lunge forward without the fear of losing occasionally. They understand that leadership is a call to a lifetime of learning and that mistakes are only opportunities to learn and make themselves better.

Great Leaders Are Effective Listeners

A good leader knows that listening holds more benefits than speaking. Becoming a leader is not a call to beat down people with your ideas and your unsolicited advice; it may even turn out that your employees know more about various issues than you do. Therefore, endeavor to give everyone attention, especially to your customers, employees, and other stakeholders.

Listening is one of the keys to building effective communication, and when you can communicate with your employees effectively, building trust becomes easier. Better communication also allows you to sell them your dream and vision, and if you listen to their feedback, you may add some important points or notice some errors in your plans. When you do this, employees will not be afraid to let you know when things are not going as you had hoped once your projects kickoff. Therefore, endeavor to be a good listener, particularly one who doesn't give emotional responses to everything he hears.

Accepts Responsibility

It is not unusual to come across a narcissistic leader who takes all the credit when the company projects go well, but blames his team when things fail to go. A good leader ought to take responsibility for everything, the good and the bad. He should be able to confess that he was mistaken. Dwight Eisenhower said that a leader's duty should consist of nothing but taking responsibility for all things that go wrong. When things go well, the leader should be careful to give all credit to the subordinates. Therefore, a leadership position is a call to serve others, carry their burdens, and inspire them to do the right things.

Builds Relationships

The responsibility of building relationships does not entail being buddies with all people, and that would not even be a wise thing to do. However, the leader is obliged to form positive, respectful relationships with all people. He does not have to interact with them on a friendship level, and they have to know that he is approachable in case there is a need for communication.

Leaders Celebrate

A good leader celebrates every ounce of achievement that his employees make; he does not wait until they have made some ground shaking earth-tottering achievement. He understands that the little things count, and therefore, there is a need for small celebrations. Celebrations could take the form of appreciation and recognition in meetings, monetary rewards, promotions, gifts, and responsibility. When the leader shows appreciation continually, he can continually push his team to perform better.

Smart leaders celebrate, particularly when things are not going too well. At this time, your team will be sulking, indifferent and beaten. That is the time to acknowledge their efforts or progress and to encourage them that there are more victories to be won ahead. This lifts their spirits and gets them back on track toward the fulfillment of organizational goals.

Chapter 4 Manipulations in Dark Psychology

Manipulation is the crucial point in Dark Psychology, which aims at changing the perception and behavior of the subject. The manipulator uses various tactics to improve the thinking of the subject towards a particular situation, thing, person, or matter. Manipulators use different tactics like persuasion, brainwashing, and blackmailing to influence others to obey them.

The layman needs to know about manipulations that every one of you would have faced in your life. The manipulator's intention could be to get benefit from the subject or to harm him. The drawback of manipulation is that the manipulator does not care about the feelings and needs of the individual. Manipulators don't care about the subjects whether they get harmed physically or emotionally. They control others' minds by blackmailing or threatening them or whatever is necessary to overpower others.

Many times, subjects recognize that they are being manipulated, but they do not consider it as the form of tactic used to control or harm them.

Some people consider manipulation as a way of leading a successful life. In this regard, manipulators use a set of manipulations and tricks to overpower the subject. Some of these techniques/manipulations are as follows:

1. Lying

Manipulators are involved in false stories, exaggerations, or partial truths. They hide the real side of the story from the subject to make him comply with them. For example, brands usually provide false statements about their product services, which they do not offer in reality.

2. Rotating the Truth

Manipulators spin the facts to match with their views. This is often done by the politicians who twist the truth to best fit their policies and rules. Manipulators in this type of tactic justify their statements by providing fake justifications and clarifications. They spin the statements to match their ideas or views even when they do not involve any original basis.

3. Withdrawal of Affection

Manipulators often persuade people by withdrawing friendship and love from the subject. In this way, they mentally torture the subject and make him comply with them. This happens in a romantic relationship when any of the partners do not comply with others. When any of the partners no longer engages in affection, love, or compliance, the other may automatically adapt to the habits and behaviors that the manipulator wants him to exhibit.

4. Sarcastic Jokes

The influencer uses sarcastic jokes over his subject in front of others to show them how powerful he is. Negative and mean comments are given to the subject in front of everyone to show the manipulator's power. Many individuals want to avoid these negative and sarcastic comments in front of everyone often engage in the behavior that the manipulator wants them to exhibit.

5. Make Subject Feel Helpless

Innocent people often are the victim of this type of tactic. Manipulators make the subject feel helpless for his lousy life. At the helplessness stage, when the influencer thinks that he is helpless and there is no one to share his problems or whatsoever. At that point, the influencer come as the helper of the individual. Then influencer takes advantage of the helplessness of the subject and makes the victim obey him.

6. Use of Aggression

To show dominance and power over individuals, the manipulator uses aggression as a tool to take control over others. The manipulator engages in aggression, the temper outburst to frighten the intended person. Thus, the individual becomes frightened and focuses more on controlling the manipulator's anger instead of talking about the original issue.

7. Plays the Role of Victim

The manipulator at this level swaps the part and acts as a victim to gain others' sympathies. He goes to the intended person and gains his sympathies in this way. The individual automatically gets inclined towards the needs and demands of the manipulator and fulfills his desires. This is the most widely used influencing technique by pretenders.

8. Pretending Ignorance

In this type of tactic, the influencer does not want to let you know what they want. The manipulator will pretend that he is ignoring the individual. This is done to divert the attention of the individual toward the manipulator. The individual at some time will comply with the manipulator to make him pay attention.

9. Threats

One of the most frequently used influencing tactics is abusing and punishing others. The influencer often involves in aggressive behaviors and threats the individual. Moreover, the influencer punishes the individual to overpower him and make him obey. Many times, the influencer involves physical violence, mental abuse, and many other punishing behaviors.

10. Emotional Blackmailing

Emotional blackmailing is another manipulating technique that the influencer uses to overpower the individual. The manipulator might trap the individual by emotionally blackmailing them that they are selfish and don't care about what's going on in the influencer's life. The tactic helps the influencer trap the individual better and make him anxious and confused.

11. Pretending Empathy

As you all know, influencers or manipulators don't usually empathize people, but if they do so it is for their good. They pretend as if they love or empathize with the individual, but in fact, they do not. This helps pretenders incline individual towards him. This is a great tactic to make someone obey you in a very sound and calm manner.

12. Positive Reinforcement

As you know, gifts and presents are considered a sign of love and charm for everyone. Gifts enhance and change the thinking pattern of the individual toward the giver. Positive reinforcement is a technique used by many people; it involves giving gifts, favorite toys, money, and many other favorites of the person. For example, parents give favorite sports car to their child upon graduating with good grades; teachers give gifts to their students when they do homework or tasks efficiently.

13. Minimization

This tactic is used to minimize the effect of manipulators' wrongdoings. Manipulators try to convince the individual that what they did wasn't as harmful or bad as it seemed to be. However, when an individual makes the manipulator confront his wrong deeds, the manipulator might consider it as the over exaggeration or overreaction from the individual. In other words, minimization involves the reduction of the adverse effects of the manipulator's wrongful acts.

Chapter 5 How to Make Friends and Influence Others

The ability to get along with people ensures success in almost any field of activity. If your work involves the need for joint discussion, team leadership, and other forms of mutual dependence, you certainly need to be able to communicate. However, this skill is necessary for everyone, both in a narrow family circle and in a wide social sphere. The means or mechanism of interpersonal communication, ensuring its normal course and productivity, is given the name "rapport." A good rapport with another person creates suitable conditions for an effective exchange of thoughts and opinions. This is necessary for trade, after contracts, at interviews, consultations, and in all other forms of active development of relationships.

The ability to communicate is not limited to the content of our words and gestures. It implies a more complex and not always noticeable interaction. Sometimes, rapport is established as if by itself, and in these cases, we could call the formula for success a good "combination of characters": you simply instantly "find a common language" with a person. You can, however, come up against the opposite: a poor combination of characters. In these cases, you may want to stay away from this person, only this is not always possible, especially when it comes to relationships, in the family, or at work. In any case, with this approach, you risk missing out on a potentially meaningful relationship.

Using NLP, you can move on to a more mature and professional approach. By becoming a master of effective communication, you will gain more power over your relationship and the results achieved. You will still enjoy natural rapport (for example, when communicating with an old friend), learn how to maintain and value such rapport without feeling the need to improve it. On the other hand, you will be able to use NLP techniques to set rapport in a wide variety of circumstances, especially in cases where it may not occur naturally.

Success often requires convincing others of the viability of their point of view: to influence, persuade, or influence to achieve change. Of course, any goals directly related to **communication** should satisfy some basic principles, which we talked about and we will continue touching the subject in other sections of this book. However, other goals may also require the ability to communicate (perhaps to achieve intermediate results on the way to the final goal). Combined with the various result checks, effective rapport installation techniques will help you communicate better and achieve more.

Fine Tuning

Usually, we like those who are *like* ourselves. It's easier to get along with such people—that is, communicate more effectively. In turn, these people also like us — for the same reason. Thus, a good rapport implies conformity, tuning. Those who are in rapport tend **to behave similarly.** Today we will tell you how to set rapport. You can begin to apply these simplest tuning techniques in just a few minutes. Other techniques require more developed skills and certain efforts to acquire them, which are often paid off by subsequent practice: thousands of NLP adherents use these tuning techniques, making sure from personal experience that they are extremely useful for setting rapport.

To improve, you first need to learn how to determine when rapport occurs and when rapport disappears. This skill involves the development of "receptivity," sensitivity to what is happening to you and others. Such skills can serve as an example of what NLP calls **unconscious competency** as some use it with ease and perfection. The basis of normal communication is, among other things, those skills that, at first glance, seem innate. You can find examples of this in commerce, contracting, consulting, and other areas of interpersonal communication. At first, mastering these skills may seem like hard work requiring great concentration, but unconscious competence in any field (for example, the ability to drive a car) always comes with experience. To learn how to achieve sustainable rapport, you need to try to **do** it. In Chapter one we gave some guidelines to build a successful rapport.

Understanding what happens when you install rapport will allow you **to choose the** most mobile and appropriate behavior. You will be able **to enter** into the communication of your own choice and not just rely on unconscious skills. Learning to drive a car, you filter out the wrong skills and develop the right ones. The same thing happens when mastering communication skills. At times, it may seem to you that you are losing some skills and mastery, but overall results will show that you are really learning more effective techniques over a long period.

The ability to establish rapport benefits not only in the field of professional activity. It can have a beneficial effect on your goals, especially if they are related to communication. The secret lies in tuning. You can set a rapport, seeking an adjustment in several ways:

　1. Physiology: posture and body movement

2. Voice: tone, the pace of speech, and other characteristics

3. Language and way of thinking: the dictionary used and the corresponding "presentation system" (vision, hearing, sensations)

4. Beliefs and values: what people believe in and what they consider important

5. Personal experience: the search for a common foundation in professional activities and interests
6. Breathing: a subtle, but very powerful means of adjustment

Setting a Rapport Using Tuning

Each adjustment method will be examined by us in turn and analyzed in sufficient detail so that you can begin to apply these techniques in everyday life. First, however, you need to understand some of the key tuning issues.
First of all, never forget how important it is to respect the tact and show respect for the interlocutor. Do not dramatically change the pose or intonation, as well as copy his gestures. Make any changes you need gradually and as inconspicuously as possible. Try not to draw the interlocutor's attention to the language of your body movements, but do your best to ensure that he also subconsciously sets up a rapport. Otherwise, you risk annoying him, hitting him, and even insulting him—and of course, then there is no question of any rapport. Although when establishing a rapport, you will first have to keep track

of each of your actions—with time, they will become laid-back and completely natural. Moreover, your respect for the interlocutor as one of the many unique individuals should be sincere, especially in those cases when his behavior and manners are different from yours.

Secondly, your respect for your own body should be just as sincere. We all stand and sit each in our way. Our other usual gestures are very different. This means that in some cases you will experience obvious inconvenience when trying to adjust, and the interlocutor will notice this. You may encounter circumstances in which deviation from the usual posture and gestures is already physically almost impossible.

When dealing with a stranger (for example, a new potential buyer), you can easily hide from him that your behavior is not typical for you in this case, but anyone who knows you well enough will certainly notice that you "left roles, "and this alone will destroy the rapport that you would be able to establish if you behaved as usual. Hence, try to stay in the "comfort zone," that is, within the natural boundaries of your personality. This does not mean that you will not be able to adapt to your interlocutor—just choose those behavioral features that will help you to adapt to your convenience or only partially.

Adjustment to Physiology

People who get along well with each other tend to take similar poses when communicating. Take a look at those absorbed in the conversation, and you will notice that their silhouettes often look like mirror reflections. After many years of marriage, older spouses often look alike.

The similarity is manifested not only in the general posture of the body, but also in gestures and manners. For example, both interlocutors can sit back and clasped their hands behind their heads or with their legs or arms crossed. Such imitation occurs quite naturally, and we hardly notice it. When rapport is established, our interests are focused on the interlocutor and the content of the conversation and not on external signs. Such a physiological adjustment serves as evidence of rapport, which means that it can be measured or **calibrated.** The physiological adjustment can be used not only for measuring rapport, but also for its installation and subsequent fixing. To adjust to the interlocutor, you can:

- Sit or stand in the same position, change your posture, or bow your head to one side;

- Cross or, on the contrary, free arms or legs; and

- Repeat his gestures with the movements of the hands, head, and body.

Partial Adjustment

Adjustment is carried out sequentially. You do not have to instantly start repeating the body language of the interlocutor in full detail. Start with one trait — say, a common posture or posture — then gradually adjust to the tilt of the head, cross your legs, reproduce the movements of the hands, the scope of gestures, the volume level and pitch of the voice, and so on. Tuning is a continuous process, not a one-time action. This means that by gaining experience and developing your skills,

you can conduct experiments with partial fine-tuning at any level.
If the interlocutor has adopted a completely inimitable or too peculiar pose, then, for adjustment, you only need to *partially* change the position of the body instead of bringing this movement to the end. To set up and save a rapport, you don't have to imitate your interlocutor exactly. For example, you may prefer a partial adjustment in the following circumstances:

- At the beginning of communication, to establish and measure rapport;
- In those cases, when fine-tuning takes you out of the "comfort zone" (see the example above);

- When the interlocutor is characterized by increased emotionality, which is reflected in the language of his body;

- In those cases, when the language of physiology is too unusual, and the interlocutor may notice that you imitate him;

- When a satisfactory rapport is already established, and you just need to save it; and

- At the first practical attempts at tuning.

What about facial expressions? If a person actively uses facial expressions — raises his eyebrows, rolls out or rolls his eyes, puffs his lips and so on — it is hardly easy for him to communicate with a passive, not betraying his feelings interlocutor, whose face is impenetrable, as if he is playing poker. People expect a similar reaction, and for such an interlocutor, the response in the form of facial expressions will seem quite normal. You will soon find that such facial expressions are difficult to fake, so stay in your "comfort zone," that is, do not adjust to the facial expressions exactly, repeat it only partially.

When adjusting to overly noticeable posture features — for example, crossed legs or arms — some delay helps. You need to wait for some time and make adjustments so that these movements look completely natural.

You can use the option of partial adjustment — the so-called "cross-adjustment": if the interlocutor folds his hands on his chest, you cross your legs, and vice versa; if he twists his fingers, you can just put his palms together; if he rubs his hands, you shuffle with your foot, and when the interlocutor crumbles a plastic cup in his hand, click the pen button. As with partial tuning, in these cases, you are not trying to accurately reproduce the actions of another person. Such actions most often require large-scale and small-scale physiological adjustment at both, the macro and micro levels. However, it may require great care to notice some of them.

Macro Fine Tuning

For fine-tuning, first of all, pay attention to your overall interlocutor's location in relation to the others. For example, if a person sits on the other side of the table or in a chair opposite, you can adjust to him as if you are looking in a mirror. On the other hand, you can sit next to him and look in the same direction, but at the same time adjust to his gestures and body position. In this case, most likely, you will be able to achieve a sense of unity and community, because you literally ended up with this person "on one side." However, at the same time, you are likely to experience difficulties when trying to establish eye contact and monitor the interlocutor's body language.

In this case, you may prefer to position the chairs at a right angle: you and your interlocutor "look in the same direction," and at the same time you can maintain eye contact or simply look together at one object.

A "work" notebook or any kind of document that helps to focus attention helps to establish rapport. Such an object becomes a neutral reference point, common support for both interlocutors.

You will only strengthen the rapport if you start vying to make notes and edits in one notebook. At the same time, you will get the opportunity to adapt not only to the physiology of the interlocutor, but also to his habit of drawing little characters or explanatory diagrams when communicating. Pass the pen to each other, mark something in the diagram one by one, or add an action plan to the items — this also helps to establish rapport.

Such simple tricks can achieve real unanimity in thoughts because communication means the ability to get closer to a person, not only in physical space.

The difference in heights also matters. Tuning is aimed at winwin rapport, not manipulation or domination. The difference in levels by elementary physical height (for example, standing and sitting) may turn out to be an incorrect signal, so this parameter must be taken into account when adjusting. If your interlocutor walks back and forth during the conversation, and you are spread out in a low chair at the other end of the room, it is unlikely that you will be able to establish a rapport. In this case, you should either join the interlocutor's mobile style or achieve at least a partial adjustment — just get out of the chair. Take into account not only body language and gestures but also all the macro aspects of tuning.

Micro Fine Tuning

The depth of adjustment forms a continuous spectrum of particulars. The same applies to trim types. For example, with good **micro-tuning,** subtle physiological changes are taken into account. Although this adjustment requires keen observation, with its help, you can seamlessly achieve powerful rapport. By carefully observing a person, you will very soon begin to notice numerous individual characteristics, each of which can turn into an effective means of setting rapport. The interlocutor does not notice the characteristic signs of his behavior, especially at the micro-level; in the same way, he will not notice your actions aimed at tuning — however, the rapport itself can be installed without any difficulties.

Some of these tricks may seem strange and even unnatural, but fine-tuning really helps to establish rapport. And what happens if the interlocutor notices your efforts to adapt to him? First of all, this happens very rarely. If this happened, then you most likely violated one of the described rules, left your "comfort zone," or forgot about the need to comply with all tact.

What if you have to communicate with someone who is also familiar with tuning techniques? This sometimes happens among businessmen and consultants. An interesting pattern is revealed here: most often, such an interlocutor will treat your professional communication skills with great respect. Ultimately, as we already know, the adjustment does not imply manipulation of the interlocutor, but the ability to better understand him and thus achieve a mutually beneficial result.

Adjustment to the Voice

Sometimes (for example, during a telephone conversation, when you do not see the interlocutor), the physiological adjustment will be impossible or inappropriate.
However, the pitch and tone of your voice also constitute an important parameter of communication. According to many studies, the voice itself often has a greater impact than spoken words. In any case, the more parameters you take into account when tuning, the more effective the rapport you set. This means essence, you need to try to understand the interlocutor and adapt to him in all areas, in all respects.
The individual characteristics that you can identify in the interlocutor's voice include:

- *Volume* (How does he say loud or quiet?)

- *Tempo* (Fast or slow?)

- *Rhythm* (Can you catch a single melody in his words? Perhaps he utters them jerkily, in staccato rhythm?)

- *Height* (What voice does he have, high or low?)

- *Timbre* (What features does he have in his voice? Is he voiced or hoarse?)

- **Intonation** (What feelings does the interlocutor emphasize with his voice?)
- **Pronunciation** (Does the interlocutor use any characteristic words or dialectical expressions Considerations?)

As usual, start by adjusting to one characteristic, and then, as you gain experience, complement it with others. First of all, do not forget about the content of the conversation. Rapport is a bit like a dance. Make any changes as naturally and invisibly as possible. Remember that you should not be too distant from your comfort zone.

Do not try to imitate dialect pronunciation and peculiarities of diction — the interlocutor may think that you are mimicking him! On the other hand, try to adapt to the general level of conversation (as occurs when communicating with a child or person much older than you) and his style (in terms of formal logical clarity).

Chapter 6 How to Persuade Some One of Your Opinion

People will not do your bidding unless you convince them otherwise. The process of convincing is not as easy as saying a few magic words; it takes hard work. Although manipulating people to do what you want is not unethical, you can only manipulate them for so long before one of them catches on and breaks from your hold. From there, the rest will begin to pull away also, one by one.

The secret to getting the same results without much resistance is to convince people. Convince them so that they take up your will as theirs or change their minds to agree to your reasoning. You only have to present your ideas and requests in the right way and watch to see whether your target will catch bait. Although there is no guarantee that your methods will work, you can take up a few tips to increase your chances of success.

Let the Structure of Your Request Be in Optimal Order

When we want something from someone, we begin by buttering the person before making our requests known. The problem with this approach is that it makes everything you said seem dishonest.

Suppose you want your friend to accompany you to an event as your date. One way to send in the request is as follows:
Hey Andrew,

It's been quite a while since I saw you. I hope all is well. I was to buy you dinner sometime last month, but I forgot, probably because I have been quite busy working on a particular project at work. I will let you in on the project when we meet. I have been invited to a charity event aimed at raising money to be used in the protection of endangered animal species, and I was hoping you would come along as my date. It will be fun. Please let me know if you can make it. I
am looking forward to seeing you.

Thanks!

[Me]

All the pleasantries and the buttering all amount to nothing because they preempt a request. Andrew will see that you are saying all these good sentiments just because you want him as a date to your event and not because you mean it. Now, let's see the same letter, structured differently.   Hey Andrew

I recently got an invitation to a charity dinner to raise money to protect endangered animal species and was wondering if I could bring you along as my date. I enjoy your company and wouldn't think of anyone else with whom I share interests and exciting conversations. I haven't seen you in a while, and I remember that I promised to take you out for dinner. Unfortunately, a project I have been handling at work has kept me glued to my computer, and I cannot find time to socialize. I will catch you on the project when we meet. Please let me know if you can make it.
I look forward to seeing you.
Thanks!

[Me]

In the second example, the pleasantries sound sincerer and heart-felt because you first made your intentions known, then went on to the buttery stuff. It proves that the best way to get someone to do what you want is to ask. Let them know how awesome they are afterward. If you take this approach, people are likely to receive your requests with some warmth.

Give Them A Chance to Speak

Has anyone ever convinced you to do anything by smacking you around or bulldozing their opinions on you? The answer to that is a definite 'no.' even if they made you do it, probably because they have authority over you, in your head, you utterly disagreed with what they were doing and were still adamant in our beliefs. You must also have been resentful and irritated by the other party. That is what happens when you force your opinions on others. People turn away and abandon you. If your goal was to convince them, you would have failed miserably.

The good news is that there is a more effective method and it's simple. It entails listening intently to what the other person is saying, and if possible, let them lay down their opinions first. As soon as they are done, now move in with your opinion, remembering to acknowledge theirs first.

Match Their Reasoning

When it comes to persuasion, it turns out that 'fighting fire with fire' is an effective persuasion technique. Experts say that borrowing from the other party's type of reasoning is more effective in persuading them than taking a whole different approach. If the other party is basing his ideas on logic, use logic too and if they are based on emotions, give an emotional argument as well.

If you are unsure about where the other party's argument is leaning towards, whether to the emotional or the logical side, here are some words to help you figure that out:

Emotional reasoning words include: imagine, suppose, intuit, believe, feel, suspect, and guess. Logical reasoning words include conclude, analyze, determine, discover, hypothesize, calculate, compel, predict, gauge, validate, think, verify, reveal, and find.

Present Your Counterargument

When trying to convince someone, always be ready to present a counterargument to the points the other party raises. Do not only present those that favor your side; create others for their side also against your argument.

It sounds counterproductive, but research has proven that twosided arguments are more effective than one-sided arguments. What this means is that you stand a better chance of convincing the other party when your argument factors in opinions from both sides than when your argument leans towards your side alone.

You do not need to support the points you raise from the other side; the secret here is to present a counterargument against them. Otherwise, if you keep supporting them, your side will lose in the debate.

Consider the following example. Let's say you are marketing makeup products to a potential buyer. You could say, "Our makeup package does not come with individual brushes, which is something I know you would be interested in."

When you say that, you will have laid out all your cards on the table and even considered something that the client would be interested in. The fact that you have told this information, even when it does not favor your side, makes you look credible. However, don't leave matters at that, go ahead and offer some follow-up information in your favor.

You could say, "Instead, we choose to offer a range of facial cleansing and scrubbing creams from which the client can choose a bottle of each. We find that most clients like to choose the quality of makeup brushes they like, which makes our range of quality creams a better choice for our package." Since you already have earned the client's trust, your explanation will have more impact than if you had waited for them to take notice of the missing brushes. It helps if you bring up a point that the client would not have brought up to support their side. Although that would also be counterproductive, it will boost your trustworthiness by making you appear more trustworthy and well informed in your field. After that, dismantle that counterargument and raise the banner of your side. The client will follow you.

Adjust the Speed of Your Speech to The Audiences

Ever had a salesman knocking at your door? There is a reason why he talks so damn fast. In some situations, talking fast gets the job done. However, in others, it doesn't.

Studies show that the way to convince your audience is to read his mind and adjust your speaking speed to the side he will likely lean towards. If you suspect that your audience will agree with your position, speak slower. If you suspect that your audience will disagree with the position you have taken, speak faster.

The reason behind the speech variations is that when your audience is likely to disagree with you, speaking very fast denies them time to come up with a counterargument, giving you a better chance of convincing them. On the other hand, if the other party is inclined to agree with you, speaking slowly gives them ample time to evaluate your arguments and come up with a few supporting arguments as well. The combination of their initial bias, your sentiments, and their new thoughts will most likely lead to them being convinced.

The conclusion to this point is that if your audience agrees with you, speak slowly; if they do not, talk fast, if they are neutral or indifferent, talk quickly so that you can hold their attention.

Chapter 7 How to Put Your Views Across to Someone in Authority

Amazingly, expressing your feelings and needs will either strengthen or wreck the relationships you have with those around you.

In life, you will have needs you want met, or emotions you want addressed, and what will determine your success in having your issues resolved is how you express yourself. If you express yourself in an off-putting way, people will turn away from you and decline to help, but if you express yourself calmly, they will be drawn to you and be open to helping you. Therefore, knowing how to express yourself correctly is vital if you want to have sustainable relationships with those around you.

When angry, it is typical of you to feel like you want to explode and equally hurt those that hurt you. Sometimes, you even end up hurting others without meaning to in your quest to assert yourself, your needs, and your boundaries. However, this is not the way to do it. You can express your anger more productively by calming down, taking time to understand your angry feelings, and then communicating your emotions in a less likely way to hurt other people. Do the same when expressing your needs so that you do not leave a trail of hurt in your quest to have your needs met.

The proper way to share your feelings most often begins with two words: "I feel…" You must be able to fill the blank space with a word that describes a feeling. For example, you could be sad, happy, disappointed, exhausted, hungry, thirsty, confused, or any other emotion you may have. You must place a name to what you are feeling. If you are having trouble doing that, try placing the feeling in one of the following four major feelings: sad, angry, scared, or glad.

One grievous mistake people make when trying to express themselves is to fill the blank space with the word 'that.' They say, "I feel that…" This is erroneous because the word 'that' is indicative that the words that follow describe a thought rather than a feeling. It is okay to share your thoughts, but in comparison to emotions, thoughts give very shallow information while feelings come from deep within and have a stronger bonding impact.

Another mistake people make is that they use another person as the originator of the feelings rather than themselves. For example, too often, you will hear someone say, "You make me feel…" instead of beginning that statement with "I feel…" You see, addressing the other person only opens the door for arguments and debates as the other party tries to save skin by pointing back the responsibility for how you feel to yourself. Here are the five reasons why you shouldn't start your selfexpression with "You make me feel…" The first reason is that it sounds like a statement of guilt and accusation rather than an account of your feelings. The second reason is that such a statement takes away your right to control your emotions and gives someone else the right to control how you feel. The third reason is that it opens the door to counteraccusations, because the other party will surely attack you as well.

The fourth reason is that it takes the focus off you and puts it on another person while you should be working on understanding yourself. Lastly, statements like these are often a result of a misunderstanding of what triggered your feelings. A person cannot make you feel anything (no one has that kind of power); you allow yourself to feel whatever you are feeling.

Communicating Your Views and Needs Effectively

As we discuss self-expression, you must take note of the role culture plays in self-expression. In some cultures, people take a direct approach when expressing their feelings, while in others, communication takes the indirect route. The direct communication style is sometimes thought to be harsh and rude, while the indirect method is perceived to be the 'nicer' way of doing things because it keeps you from hurting other people's feelings.

When angry or when you urgently need your needs met, it would seem that the conversation structure no longer matters because all that the individual demands are the results. While doing this could get you what you want, it tears apart relationships and friendships already established. However, here's what you should be doing instead:

1. Become Aware of What Is Going on Inside You

If you are raging mad, be still. This is not the time to express your emotions because, in your quest to express all that you feel, whether in a one-on-one conversation, a phone call, text messages or an email, your message is likely to come out harsher and meaner than you anticipated. The reason is that when you are overcome with anger, that is all your mind will think about, and logic will not have an opportunity to show up. Therefore, when angry, pump your brakes until you have cooled off, then you can see clearly, think logically, and communicate effectively.

Staying at the same spot will not calm you down; you need some distraction, something that can take your mind off what is happening. You could take a walk, watch funny videos on Facebook or YouTube, pray, meditate, or exercise. Hobbies are also a good way to distract yourself. You could cook, swim, draw, bake, write, or do whatever else lifts your spirits. Do any activity that will help you regain your peace, and allow you to see things clearly.

2. Talk Yourself Through What Is Going On

After you have calmed down, it helps to think about and talk to yourself about the situation rationally. Your reasoning should always take a higher position in your life, higher than your emotions. You see, feelings are sometimes wrong because you have interpreted a situation with your emotions, while rational thinking brings out the sense of what is happening. Feelings can be wrong, but rarely is rationality. Therefore, although you may not feel like you want to think about the situation and keep a positive dialog going on in your mind, do it because you need the peace it brings.

Take a situation where your boss is always asking you to work during the weekends, but you would rather spend the weekend with your children. His requests would make you understandably angry because you should be relaxing during the weekend. However, instead of speaking to your boss, lashing out and possibly declaring that you do not need the job anymore (which you do), be calm and think about how you will present your needs in an assertive manner.

Once you are calmer, tell him that you find it difficult working during the weekend because you feel that the weekend allows you to bond with your children because you hardly ever get any time or chance during the weekdays. See if he can find someone else to cover the weekend shifts and let him know what a pleasure it always is when he considers you for additional roles. Let him know that if there is anything you can do to help, you would be willing to do it anytime during weekday business hours. An approach like this would prove to your boss that you value your work and respect his leadership. Another person could have approached the boss talking about their job description at the time of hire and how there was nothing in it saying they would be working on the weekends. A conversation like it would have made the boss angry, and the next logical step would have been to throw the person out, however productive the person is.

Always remember that feelings sometimes supersede job performance. If you are always making your boss angry but are good at your job, the boss will not be tolerant of you for too long. If, on the other hand, you are always making your boss happy, he may be patient with you and get your assistance to help you improve your performance. Therefore, endeavor to make people in authority happy with you. Do not be a sycophant; be respectful and work diligently.

3. See If You Have Misplaced Blame

Placing blame on a person or a situation for how you feel feels good. If you are hungry, unhappy, overworked, stressed, and tired, it feels good to have someone or something you can point to as the origin of those feelings. However, what this does is alienate the people involved. No one likes to be looked at as the source of some sadness or frustration, and when you do it, you drive them away. When they go, things become worse, and the more frustrated you will be. You will even be more frustrated because the people you drove away were not the real cause of your problem.

4. Look Beyond Yourself

Focusing on your emotions and the reasons behind them will have you looking within yourself and fixing all your attention on yourself. Experts confirm this, saying that negative emotions cause people to become self-centered.

One thing that can get you out of your mind is curiosity. Be curious to know why a person is behaving the way he is. Be genuinely interested in knowing the emotions a person is going through, and instead of confronting them harshly, seek to understand why the individual did what he did. You see, most people do not hurt others willingly; they do it accidentally, by mistake. Sometimes, they are not even aware that their deeds have caused you so much hurt and grief. Before you assign blame, seek to know the story on the other side.

5. Be Accommodating

Accommodation, in this case, means that you ought to make room for another person's needs, opinions, and even mistakes. When you make room, you seek to know the reason behind their behavior rather than just assuming the worst and making your conclusions. You also show that you respect the other party's feelings, thoughts, and the right to hold a perspective different from yours.

The result will be that you become more understanding and can build a deeper relationship based on compassion, communication, civility, and empathy. A civil approach, rather than an aggressive one, allows the other party to become more accommodating of your perspective and encourages them to open up so that they open up to you.

6. Communicate with Skill

When you share your feelings, needs, and perspective, begin by using the word 'I' then follow it up with what you want to say. However, don't stop there, lest you encourage selfcenteredness in you. Ask the other party to share their perspective too, and examine it with sincerity. Be genuinely interested in what other people are feeling, and together you can work toward a compromise.

For example, if you are hungry, try to know if the other party is hungry too, and if he or she is, you could walk into a restaurant and share a meal. If you are aggravated by something, see if the other party feels the same way, and discuss how you can both contribute to making the situation better, where possible. The result of this kind of interaction is that the two parties will be drawn towards each other and start to care for each other, even when they have opposing views.

Chapter 8 Influence People With Principles of Persuasion

Some people are naturally quite influential and can get others to do what they want. Being able to influence others might seem like a beautiful gift. Well, the good news is anyone can learn about influencing others and develop the skill. In this section you will learn about a couple of simple principles of influence you can easily use in your daily life.

Reciprocity

Reciprocity is a form of exchange conducted for the benefit of all the parties involved. Reciprocity is an inherent trait present in all humans. This is one of the reasons why the likelihood of others saying yes to any request you make increases exponentially when you first give them something. It primarily works along the lines of, "If you scratch my back, then I will scratch yours."

This is based on the quid pro quo principle, a Latin expression that means "something for something." If you have watched the movie the "Silence of the Lambs," you would remember Hannibal Lecter telling Clarice Starling, an FBI agent, that he would exchange the information he has if she gave him some information in return. He was expecting reciprocal treatment. For instance, if you go out with your friend and pay for a meal, your friend might offer to foot the bill the next time you go out. If a person receives a gift, service, or even a specific behavior first, his likelihood of reciprocating is quite high because he will feel obliged.

Consistency

Robert Cialdini believes that the principle of unity and commitment are related to one's self-image. It is about a person's inherent desire to ensure that their beliefs and behaviors are consistent with their self-image and values. Humans like to be compatible with the things they have previously done or said. Consistency is triggered by asking and looking for any small commitments. It relies on the influence of active, public, and any voluntary commitments which people make. Whenever someone makes a public commitment, their desire to stick to the word increases.
The first aspect of this principle deals with making an active commitment. An active involvement usually occurs whenever someone says something to others. It can be in the form of a spoken or written word. If a person says that he will start doing something is the first step, but his chances of following through are greater when he actively commits to it. The next part of this principle deals with committing a public one. When there are witnesses to this commitment, it creates a sense of

accountability. No one likes going back on their word, especially when others are aware of it. The third part of this principle is all about it being voluntary. You cannot force someone to make a public commitment. Instead, it must come from within, and only then will the person stick to it. There was a simple experiment conducted to study the behavior of humans related to commitment and persuasion. In the studies conducted by researchers, it was discovered that only a few people were willing to put off large wooden signs on the front yard to show their support for the "Drive Safely" campaign (The Six Principles of Persuasion by Dr. Cialdini, 2019). However, in the same neighborhood, there were four times as many residents who were inclined to set up the same signs. Why does this difference arise? All this was because one set of residents had previously agreed to put up a small postcard on the front window showed their support for the Drive safely campaign. This little postcard displayed the initial commitment, which caused a 400% increase in the homeowner's willingness to put up a sign showing their support for the same cause.

For instance, if you've ever visited a doctor's clinic, you might be given a form to fill out for your follow-up appointment. If you fill this form up yourself, the chances of visiting the doctor and sticking to your appointment increase significantly.

So how can this principle be utilized? As soon as you persuade someone to do something, ensure that he or she makes a voluntary and public commitment about it.

Social Validation

Usually, the way people tend to think, feel, and act in the situation depends on the social cues they receive from others, especially their peers. If you believe someone thinks like you do or has similar opinions, your behavior might be influenced by the other person's behavior. Did you ever come across the phrase, "monkey see, monkey do"? Well, this principle of influencing others is based on this idea. A lot of people are imitators, and only a small fraction consists of initiators. So, it isn't surprising that people do things when they see others doing the same. This is one of the underlying behavioral traits used by advertisers and marketers. For instance, many social networking sites offer suggestions about pages or events that any of your followers or friends have shown their interest in. One of the most common examples of social validation can be seen while doing any shopping online. For instance, if you're purchasing a specific book on a website like Amazon, you might be more inclined to buy the book which has received good reviews from other users. Even managers regularly use this tactic to influence their team members while making any significant changes. If the manager can get one of his team members to support the move, he will increase the likelihood that his colleagues will soon follow suit. If the first person takes action, it triggers the power of social proof.

Liking

If you are ever in trouble, do you ask any of your friends or loved ones for advice? Do you listen to their opinion, or would you listen to that of a stranger? You would give preference to your friend's advice over that of a stranger. Why does this happen?
The answer is quite simple—we listen to those we like.

The chances of others following your advice will increase if they like you. This is one of the reasons why word-of-mouth publicity or recommendations work in this world. Once you build a rapport with a person and discover some common interests, your ability to influence that person will increase. This is a simple idea, and it will work brilliantly. The simplest way to use this technique is by finding shared interests or hobbies. Once you connect with someone over this, it gives you a solid head start. By observing others, you can quickly discover any cues or topics that will help you find some common ground.

Another tactic you can use is by offering genuine appreciation, praise, or compliments. Make sure that the recognition you're offering is not fake, and don't go overboard with compliments. If you give out too many respects, it will look like flattery, and flattery will not get you anywhere.

Scarcity

We all value scarce things. This is the basic idea upon which the concept of demand and supply rests. As things start to become limited, they are viewed to be more valuable. The lesson is the supply of something; the greater its value, and the demand is higher. You can easily use this principle of influence to persuade others. Owners of businesses and stores use this principle by providing certain limited-time offers or one-time deals that make the products more appealing to their target audience. Scarcity can be easily created, and it doesn't always have to be a natural scarcity. It is not just about creating a sense of poverty, but the way you present it matters. Your message will be more potent if the language you're using demonstrates what the other person will lose out on if he doesn't act or do something immediately. Instead of harping on what others can gain, tell them what they will lose if they don't act quickly. Another approach you can use while using this principle is exclusivity.

Authority

Others are more likely to listen to you when they perceive you as an expert in a specific field area. Why does this happen? Usually, experts are believed to have the necessary knowledge required to make the right decisions that others might take a long time to devise for themselves. By establishing your credibility as an expert or an authority, your ability to influence others increases. Many people tend to miss out on this opportunity because they assume others can identify their expertise by themselves. Never leave things up for interpretation, as it can be easily overlooked. There are various ways in which you can establish your credibility. The simplest way is to earn the necessary credentials in the form of degrees, diplomas, or certificates. When you display these credentials such that others can view them, they will start thinking of you as an expert. This is one of the reasons why most doctors display their degree certificates or diplomas in the offices. As soon as the patient glances upon them, it reaffirms the authority. Another simple way is to provide this information to others whenever you're conversing with them. Keep in mind that your expertise isn't something that others are always aware of, so conveying it to them is crucial. As mentioned earlier, the majority of the human population consists of followers, and they're often looking for leaders. If you have selected a well-defined niche, then becoming an authority in the niche will be quite helpful.

Once you start using the various principles of influence discussed in this section, you will notice an improvement in your ability to influence others. Use caution whenever you are attempting any of these techniques. If it becomes visibly evident to others that you're trying to change them, they will shut themselves up, and the methods will not be effective.

Chapter 9 Emotional Intelligence

Emotional intelligence involves ways to persuade others, but in a far more honest way than attempting to hijack another person's thoughts. When you act with emotional intelligence, you are acting in honest ways that truly convey your convictions. Those with emotional intelligence are those who can act in ways that people like to see. Other people naturally gravitate toward those with emotional intelligence because those with high EQs truly care about other people. They can manage their own emotions with others' emotions and have nearly perfected the juggling act between their wants and needs and the wants and needs of others. Truly passionate about others, these people are happier than most, and they have to do very little to convince the rest to help them of their own volition. Of all the types of persuasion, this is probably the most organic—it evolves on its own without the person having to tweak their behaviors. It is a natural give-and-take that comes naturally to some, but is learned by others, and it leaves everyone happier and in a better position than before.

What is Emotional Intelligence?

Emotional intelligence is another type of intelligence proposed alongside traditional intelligence, which refers to an individual's cognitive skills. The emotional intelligence quotient (EQ) is often seen alongside the intelligence quotient (IQ) when discussing an individual's overall intelligence. Ultimately, while those with a higher IQ may understand and do more, those with higher EQs are far more likely to be successful in their personal and professional lives. They can navigate society far easier than someone with a lower EQ and higher IQ, which means that they are likely to find enjoyment easier than others. They can create meaningful relationships far easier, and they tend to have the social skills necessary for successful interaction with others. Higher EQs are so incredibly valued that they are often considered far more valuable than having a higher IQ, and even employers will tend to choose the person with a higher EQ over someone with a lower EQ and higher IQ because those with the higher EQ are likely to be a better employee and coworker, even if they may not necessarily be as skilled at that particular job. Emotional intelligence is primarily a skillset. For some, they are born with the ability to be naturally emotionally intelligent. Others learn how to do it after practice. It is a mindset in which you recognize that the key to success is in first managing yourself to manage and facilitate relationships with others. It involves keying into other people's states of mind and using that empathetic understanding to aid yourself in bettering the situation for everyone rather than focusing on yourself. It is not manipulative—it involves having the other people decide entirely on their own what they want to follow, developing a natural rapport between the individual with high EQ and those around them.

Those with this skillset are happier than those who struggle with their emotions. They are more successful in their lives. They are more at ease because they know that other people legitimately have their back and are not acting out of coercion. They have the loyalty of those around them, and that loyalty was legitimately earned through their behaviors. It is deserved rather than forced or faked, and that sets those with high EQ apart from others.

Ultimately, emotional intelligence is comprised of three distinct skills. Each of these acts together to create wellrounded, natural-born leaders. People with high emotional intelligence levels are:

- **Able to identify the emotions of themselves and those around them.**

- **Able to use those emotions and apply them to problem-solving and thinking without letting the emotions sway them negatively or impulsively.**

- **Able to manage their own emotions as well as influence the emotions of those around them** —they can comfort a hysterical person or calm someone in the throes of rage.

Traits of High Emotional Intelligence

Those with high levels of emotional intelligence typically have several key traits resulting from their skills. Here are the seven most common traits shared by highly emotionally intelligent individuals. As you read through this list, try to think of how these traits would naturally lend themselves to developing a natural rapport and inspire people to help in any way the individual asks.

Self-Aware

Emotionally intelligent individuals are self-aware. They know their feelings, their strengths, and weaknesses, and they use this knowledge to their advantage. They do not mind criticisms or comments from other people, especially when it relates to their weaknesses, and they are always attempting to better themselves in ways that most people would never think possible.

Balanced

People with high emotional intelligence also tend to take care of themselves almost meticulously. They know that they are not going to be successful if they don't prioritize taking care of themselves, so they do exactly that — they prioritize themselves.
They eat well, sleep well, and exercise. When they take care of themselves, they can better take care of others.
Optimistic

The high EQ individual does not worry about failing. Even in failing, some things can be learned, and nothing is entirely useless. They always find the good in situations, whether it is treating the incident as a learning experience or finding other unforeseen consequences that can work well for them. This can be quite inspiring for others, and it allows the highly emotionally intelligent person to become quite flexible, always rolling with punches because there is some good in everything.

Empathetic

The high EQ individual is also quite empathetic. We have already discussed why empathy is important in its chapter, but to reiterate, when relying on empathy, individuals tend to lean toward helpful behaviors, even if they do not get anything in return. This enables an individual to be more successful and capable of success than someone who does not empathize well.

Inspire Change

The emotionally intelligent individual is not afraid of change—he will seek to become the catalyst for the change if he believes it is right. He knows his values, and he will act with integrity, even if he feels that what he believes is right is less popular or less supported. He will always go with his values as a guideline, and he will use those values to inspire change where he feels it's necessary.

Curious and Willing to Question

The highly emotionally intelligent individual is interested in the world around him. He wants to see how people are functioning and what makes them tick. He watches to see how situations play out and is not afraid to ask questions to understand someone else's perspective. He is happy to learn how other people think, and he will use that newfound knowledge to better assign tasks to people.

Not Afraid of Failure or Imperfection

Those with high EQs do not shy away from imperfection or failure. They understand that failure is a natural part of life, and rather than condemning it, it should be celebrating. After all, failure is just another tick on the list of things not to do—it was a learning experience, and that is valuable in its own right.

Together, all of these traits combine to create a high EQ individual. These traits make for patient, empathetic, and inspiring leaders that people will naturally gravitate toward. They will want to aid the person with a high EQ because that person will not punish them. He will listen to concerns and complaints with grace and take them into consideration. He will seek to benefit other people, empathizing closely with them, and using that empathy as a sort of feedback for himself and what he is doing. He typically cannot be easily corrupted, as he has his values that he holds in his heart. He will be happy to change plans if things are not working out without fear of admitting he is wrong, because being wrong is not something to be ashamed of. Overall, these traits combine and make for an incredibly effective leader.

The Four Emotional Intelligence Domains

In emotional intelligence, there are four major domains of skillsets that combine to create the entire intelligence. These four domains each encompass a different type of skills that build upon the skills that came before in a sort of pyramid. Selfawareness creates the foundation for self-regulation, which sets the stage for social awareness, and when all three of those skillsets combine, they can create effective relationship management.

Self-Awareness

As the most fundamental level of emotional intelligence, selfawareness focuses on the self. It is the pursuit of understanding an individual's self, as without having the fundamental knowledge of yourself, how can you hope to understand others?
Those who are self-aware can recognize and accurately label their own emotions, as well as understand their strengths and weaknesses and their values. They know themselves intimately, and they use that knowledge and understanding of

their mind to create the foundations for the rest of emotional intelligence. The skills associated with this domain include:

- **Recognizing your emotional states and how those emotional states impact other areas of your personal life.**

- **Being able to accurately identify your strengths and weaknesses.**

- **Having an accurate idea of your self-worth and what you are capable of achieving.**

Self-Regulation

Self-regulation refers to your ability to manage your own emotions. You know how to identify your emotions, and you are now beginning to ensure that your responses to those emotions are regulated into effective and beneficial ways, rather than just giving in to whatever impulse you felt. When you are skilled in self-regulation, you can identify how the outside world is making you feel, and you can handle those feelings in mature ways. You generally have a strong grasp on your behaviors and actions, and you can use that strong grasp to your advantage.

The skills associated with this domain include:

- **Being able to control emotional impulses.**

- **Being trustworthy, honest, and always acting in ways that are true to your values.**

- **Being flexible because you understand how to regulate your emotions, even in times of stress, so that everything goes smoothly.**

- **Being optimistic and recognizing that there are always opportunities to better the situation and learn from the failures.**

- **Willingness to take the initiative to trigger a change in status quo, even when your opinion is currently unpopular.**

Social Awareness

Social awareness refers to your ability to recognize, understand, and respond to what those around you need. This is often compared with good customer service—because good customer service representatives can do everything this domain encompasses. They are good at understanding their customers' needs, and they can respond to that with ease. Those skilled in social awareness are in tune with what people around them are thinking and can make other people feel at ease around them.

Here are the key skills of this domain:

- **Highly empathetic and in tune with other people's thoughts, feelings, needs, and concerns.**

- **Able to understand how interactions work within a group and what the politics of that group entail.**

- **Able to meet the needs of those around them accurately and quickly, even without prompting.**

- **Able to gain the trust of others and build rapport naturally and effectively.**

Relationship Management

The last of the four domains of emotional intelligence is relationship management. This is the skill that leaders develop and is where the most influence comes in. This domain allows for a connection to be built between yourself and others, leaving the other person feeling supported and listened to. This means that the other person feels inherently valued by you, and when the other person feels valued, he or she is more likely to follow your lead, believing that you only have the best in mind. This is the skillset that has been culminated with the previous domains of emotional intelligence in creating a well-rounded, wellrespected, and deserving leader. This domain encompasses the following skills:

- **Ability to influence others without relying on manipulation.** You use nothing but your truthful words and behaviors to show the other person why they should do what you are asking, and they typically agree and do so.

- **Ability to be an inspirational leader.** You create and follow a vision with integrity and passion, and you can motivate others to follow suit.

- **Ability to understand the strengths and weaknesses of other people and use that ability to develop the other people as well.** You provide the feedback necessary to better those around you in ways that are tactful and wellreceived.

- **Ability to recognize when change is needed,** and a willingness to be the catalyst and driving force for that change.

- **Ability to settle conflicts quickly and easily, in ways that are fair to everyone involved and that defuse the conflict without ruining relationships.**

- **Ability to create teams that work together effectively and smoothly, both personally and professionally.** You can recognize how different people's strengths can complement and support each other's weaknesses and can arrange people in a way that makes the most sense for everyone involved.

How Emotional Intelligence Influences Others

People with high emotional intelligence naturally influence others in ways that others find fair and just. They can sway people to do whatever they feel is right simply by asking others because people already respect them. This leads to many different types of successful relationships, ranging from

leaderships to partners, relationships of every kind are further bettered and built upon through high levels of emotional intelligence. Here are some of the ways people with higher EQs are more successful in several different contexts:
Emotionally Intelligent Leaders and Managers

The emotionally intelligent leader or manager can create a smooth flow between people under his charge. He sees how people interact with each other and can give every person a job that is tailored to their skillsets and competencies that help the team. He can solve conflicts before they become a problem and foster a good relationship between all team members. He is skilled in understanding what the people need, even when he has not been told, and he is widely respected for doing anything he can to help others. He often asks how he can help them and will get down and help with their work rather than telling them to hurry up and complete whatever needs to be done. He is not afraid to help them and will gladly do so, while listening to advice from those under his charge when they suggest ways, he could improve his skills and relationships with them. People respect him enough to want to do what he asks, as he has proven time and again that he only has their best interests at heart.
Emotionally Intelligent Coworkers

An emotionally intelligent coworker can manage herself well, paying attention to her interactions and ensuring she is not overstepping or bothering others. She will do her best to ensure that she completes her work to her standards, rather than just to the standard expected of her, and she will try to support others as well. She understands how to read other people, and because she does, she tends to manage her behaviors well since she can pick up on cues from others. She is generally a pleasure to be around because she balances others' needs with herself and is always happy to help when necessary. Because she is so attentive to others' needs, others usually have no problem aiding her when she feels the need to ask.

Emotionally Intelligent Partners

In a marriage or relationship, emotional intelligence can make or break the entire partnership. If one individual is not emotionally intelligent, he is likely to be aggressive and sensitive, easily swayed by emotions and passions, which makes him far more likely to say or do things he regrets when he inevitably angers his partner or her partner inevitably angers him. However, with higher EQs, the partners can work out conflicts without letting their emotions sway them into making poor decisions or saying things they regret. They can better manage the relationships and meet the needs of the other person when they can empathize more, which leads to generally happier relationships. Each person will be deeply invested in recognizing how to aid the other, and this ability to remain steadfast, not swayed by emotions, builds a deep trust and rapport within each other that allows for each to ask for what they need—and get it. The kind of influence this develops is from a deep-seated trust of each other; they know that the other person would not steer them wrong, and they will do as requested.

Emotionally Intelligent Parents

Emotionally intelligent parents often have an easier time managing the feelings of their children. They can speak to their children in ways that can defuse situations, mitigate conflicts, and show the children what the right behaviors are. They are not likely to resort to punishments, especially not first thing, and they are willing to spend the time and energy to talk through problems rather than just telling the child what to do.
Because these parents get down on the child's level and walk them through it, the children are more willing to obey. They

see that the problem is being handled with empathy and respect, and they learn to internalize and mimic that. When the parent can empathize with the child, such as providing a time they had to do something that they did not want to do, just like the child, the child is a little more receptive to completing whatever it was that the parent requested. The child is also more likely to develop problem-solving skills that will enable him to do what is necessary in the future without such a big fuss. Overall, the child sees the reasons for doing what the parent is requesting, and once the child understands the logic, the child is far more likely to obey than if the parent had simply appealed to authority and demanded obedience.

Chapter 10 Dark Manipulation Techniques

Similar to the persuasion techniques, the manipulation techniques are used to influence how another person reason and behave. When these techniques are utilized correctly, a person will have no idea that they are being manipulated. Some of the techniques are more effective once partnered with another technique, and others can stand alone. However, with every one of the proceeding techniques, it is important not to get caught.

Fear and relief focus on the manipulation of another person's emotions, which is likely to cause an immense amount of stress and anxiety, but it is also extremely effective. The method comes in two parts, hence the title of the technique. The first part centers on the idea of fear. The individual using the technique will cause another person to fear something, which brings out that person's vulnerabilities. The manipulator will then provide relief from the distress. The trickiest component of this technique is finding the best fear tactic. It is important to inflict fear based on a person's specific stressors. There must be an awareness of what to say and do to bring out an individual's vulnerabilities, but one must also be prepared with a way to replace the fear with relief.

If the technique is done correctly, the switch between fear and relief causes a person to experience mood swings. As a result, the individual will become fully exposed. An instance of how this tactic can be used in the real-world can be found in the news at home. For example, when a station begins talking about an outbreak of the flu where some cases have resulted in death, people tend to become panicked. The news comes in with statements such as "stay tuned to hear how you can protect yourself." The news provides the viewers with possible ways to keep themselves and the people they care about safe. A few other possible options are to use a personal relationship to get into a familiar mind, or bosses can use the technique to motivate employees. The technique can be used for completely selfish reasons or to influence a positive outcome as well. The second tactic is the mirroring technique and is one of the most well-known options. Similar to the previous technique, this too comes in two parts. At first, the person being manipulated is mirrored by the manipulator. The goal is to create a level of trust with the target that will hopefully allow you to go in to exploit them. During the first part of this technique, the manipulator will focus on and match the other person's body language, voice inflections, and automatic reactions. It is important to remain subtle while doing this or the person being mirrored may become wary of the behavior because if not, the trust will be lost.

The second part of this technique involves the switch in who is being mirrored. The person being manipulated begins copying the manipulator. Once this happens, it is a sign that a complete level of trust has been established. It takes a great deal of patience to reach this portion of the tactic, but once the trust is there, some of the other manipulation techniques can take over.

Studies have been conducted to prove the effectiveness of the mirroring technique. One study was done during a business negotiation. The results indicated that better deals were made when the negotiator copied their coworkers. A different study was done in a restaurant setting where waitresses received higher percentages in tips after mirroring their customers. It is important to note that when mirroring is only used for personal gain, the act can only last for so long before the person being manipulated begins seeing through the facade. The next technique uses guilt, which is a tool used to psychologically manipulate an individual. When a person is experiencing guilt, they will likely try to compensate whichever way they can. The manipulator will come in and suggest their idea for how to extinguish the guilt. The tactic is the most successful with people the manipulator has already developed a bond with, especially those who have already let the manipulator down in the past. The manipulator will influence their target by slowly and patiently planting ideas into their unconscious mind until the person being manipulated believes those desires to be their own. While this tactic appears to be simpler and easier, a manipulator can run into trouble if it becomes obvious what is happening. It is important to be careful and strategically choose the words and actions to ensure that the target will not suspect the manipulation. When the technique is done correctly, the individual will do what they can to not see as an immoral person.

Although it seems as though guilt is strictly a negative use of manipulation, there are cases of positive guilt. For example, with the downfall of the ecosystem today, companies and organizations are promoting eco-friendly products. The promotions are not shy about putting the blame where it belongs, the human race. While human beings are the cause of the attack on the environment, they are also the solution. The use of guilt, in this case, is used to try to influence people to do better and save the environment.

The fourth technique focuses on playing the victim, which is linked to the guilt approach. When a manipulator is acting like a victim, they are forcing the target to feel ashamed. The manipulator would likely use phrases such as, "Why are you treating me this way?" or "Do you treat everyone this way, or is it just me?" Once the manipulator makes accusations of mistreatment, no matter how insignificant the resistance maybe, the person being manipulated will look back at their actions or words and be influenced into believing they have been illmannered. As a result, it will be easier for the manipulator to influence the individual to do what they want. When using this approach, it is important to keep in mind that there are sometimes drawbacks if the manipulator overuses the victim card. One example of effective use of this technique is in an abusive relationship. The abuser will turn their aggressive actions around onto their victim. Say a woman was out with her friends and had forgotten to tell her partner, the abuser might strike his partner, they may suggest something like, and "You made me do it. If you had just said where you were, I wouldn't have been so worried." The abused victim would believe they had done something wrong and would attempt to make it up to their partner. In this case, guilt plays a huge factor in the outcome of the manipulation. This suggests that the guilt and the victim techniques can work separately, but when to put together, they become their most effective.

People with a narcissistic personality commonly use the manipulation technique known as "love bombing." The tactic plays heavily on an individual's emotions by showering them with affection and being attentive to their wants and needs. This takes place at the beginning of a relationship with the person being influenced. The goal is to make it difficult for the manipulated individual to not see the good in the manipulator, even though the influencer's actions are a front. The victim is tricked into an emotional trap with the manipulator, leading to an intense and overwhelming feeling of affection for the manipulator.

This technique is most effective on particular individuals, specifically those who have a deep desire for love and attention. Lonely people are also suitable targets. It is important to keep the true intentions a secret or the bond will not form between the manipulator and their victim. An example of this would be a cult. The members are overly kind and enthusiastic towards possible new members. The cult members are careful about hiding their intentions until after the proposed supporters have officially signed up as real members. After this point, it is too late to turn back because the influence has already taken over.

The sixth technique involves bribery. When a manipulator rewards an individual, that individual will feel obligated to return the favor somehow. The influencer takes advantage of their target's mental state to achieve their desires. The tactic begins with discovering the desires of their victim so that the manipulator can meet such desires. The next step is to propose a favor in return. However, if the manipulator asks for the favor in a way that sounds threatening, the manipulation ends there. It is essential to keep the conversation light and have it appeared the manipulator is simply being kind.

Bribery is believed to be the easiest manipulation technique if it is done properly. The most important component of this tactic is timing. The manipulator should give an individual what they want cautiously, and only after a substantial amount of time has passed should the manipulator collect their request. By waiting, the manipulator is establishing trust with the person they are manipulating.

When bribery is put into practice, studies have shown that many of the manipulators provide small gestures of kindness and in return, they receive a more generous reward. Bribery can also take place over a longer period of time, like providing someone with discounted items. The person being manipulated will see their manipulator as someone who has been kind multiple times in the past, suggesting they should repay the favor.

An example of the successful use of bribery is if an employee is looking for a promotion. Around Christmas time, the employee gives his boss an expensive watch, and a few months later, when the position opens up, he applies. The boss may remember the act of kindness from his employee and give him the position.

The next manipulation technique is, ironically, also a key component to any healthy relationship, being a good listener. However, the motives in manipulation are different than those for an honest relationship. For a manipulator, listening to another person is an essential component to influence them. The art of being a listener has two main benefits for manipulators.

When a manipulator appears to be interested in learning about their target, it shows a level of friendliness that translates to being trustworthy. This is especially appealing to individuals who do not have social interactions often. No matter how long the conversations or how dry the exchange is, it is important to stay alert. The information divulged at the beginning is essential for the second portion of listening.

There is a possible way to grow the trust between the manipulator and the person being manipulated so that influence can take place. If a manipulator recalls details that their target had spoken to them about, the target believes the manipulator listened to them because they truly cared about what the manipulated person had to say.

An example would be if a real estate agent listens to a client while showing them possible rental locations. When the client comes back in for a second showing, the real estate agent may bring up the family vacation the client said his family was going on. The act of listening and appearing to care may be what closes the deal for the real estate agent.

Another manipulation technique is to examine the reading of body language, both psychologically and emotionally. What a person says with their body can be more reliable than a person's actual words. It is easier to conceal the truth with words than it is with the human body because body language tends to be an involuntary reaction that a person is unaware they are doing.

Reading body language is not difficult; however, it is imperative to recognize the meaning behind different body language types. When a person has their arms crossed over their chest, this usually indicates they feel defensive or disengaging from the conversation. If an individual has their head tilted to the side, this may indicate they listen intently to the conversation. When a person has their fingertips pressed together, but their palms are apart, this signifies the person is showing signs of authority and power over others. People who stand with their back straight imply a high level of confidence. Eye contact is a tool used to create a comfortable environment. For example, in an interrogation room, a detective will read a possible suspect's body language to pick up on any sign of guilt or unease. If the suspect signals a guilty conscience, the detective will push for more information in the hopes of nailing down a conviction.

While manipulators can use body language to read a situation and a particular person's emotions, they can also use some of their body language to influence other people. Manipulators can use eye contact to ensure a level of trust from another person. A manipulator can also use standing up straight or having their fingertips together to put themselves in a place of power over someone else.

The next manipulation technique of playing with another person's feelings is an easy way to influence a him or her. The idea behind this tactic is that once a person develops a strong emotional connection, especially a loving one, it becomes easier to force them into thinking emotionally rather than rationally. As a result, a manipulator can influence a person into doing whatever they want.

The trick to achieving a type of connection is to first master one's own emotions. If a person attempting to manipulate is not in tune with their own emotions, they may run the risk of being the one who gets manipulated. Fear and sympathy are both strong sentiments that come into play during an emotional connection, and both the person being manipulated and the manipulator can fall victim to these emotions. A real-world example of this approach would be through marketing. Companies try to appeal to their loyal customers about the new products a company has produced. Apple comes out with new high-tech phones that their most loyal customers are waiting in line to pick up. Even though a person's current phone works perfectly fine, their desire for the new merchandise outweighs the brain's logical side.

The final manipulation technique is all about using a person's looks to their advantage. No matter how hard people try to deny it, good-looking and charismatic individuals are easier to trust. However, good-looks can only get a manipulator so far. It is crucial to marry the beauty with the actual strategy. The previous technique is helpful tools to couple with good-looks. Positive use of body language can promote comfort. Making a person feel special and giving a slight air of confidence is also beneficial for an attractive manipulator.

A well-known but sinister example is Ted Bundy. The serial killer was notorious for his good looks and his ability to lure a woman away before murdering them. He was a collegeeducated man with a charming smile. The man was able to take a woman in broad daylight in public places without setting off any alarm bells from people. Even after he was caught, it was difficult for police, correctional officers, and citizens to believe such an attractive man could have been behind the brutal killings. Bundy was even able to marry after being arrested for at least 30 murders. The man manipulated every person he came into contact with, but in the end, the law still won.

Chapter 11 Developing Mind Control

Mind Control

Mind control involves using influence and persuasion to change the behaviors and beliefs of someone. That someone might be the person themselves or it might be someone else. Mind control has also been referred to as brainwashing, thought reform, coercive persuasion, mental control, and manipulation, just to name a few. Some people feel that everything is done by manipulation. But if that is true or to be believed, then important points about manipulation will be lost. Influence is much better thought of as a mental continuum with two extremes. One side has respectful and ethical influences to improve the individual while showing respect for them and their basic human rights. The other side contains dark and destructive influences that work to remove basic human rights from a person, such as independence, the ability for rational thought, and sometimes their total identity. When thinking of mind control, it is better to see it as a way to use influence on other people that will disrupt something in them, such as their way of thinking or living. Influence works on the very basis of what makes people human, such as their behaviors, beliefs, and values. It can disrupt the very way they chose personal preferences or make critical decisions. Mind control is nothing more than using words and ideas to convince someone to say or do something they might never have thought of saying or doing on their own.

Mind control uses the idea that someone's decisions and emotions can be controlled using psychological means. It is using powers of negotiation or mental influence to ensure the outcome of the interaction is more favorable to one person over the other. This is basically what marketing is: convincing someone to do something particular or buy something in particular. Being able to control someone else's mind merely means understanding the power of human emotion and being able to play upon those emotions. It is easier to have a mental impact on people if there is a basic understanding of human emotions.

Many forms of mind control are considered to be rooted in dark psychology because many believe that mind control is an impure strategy used by those who cannot be bothered to do things themselves. They believe that it is a form of evil hence why it is called "dark" psychology. While we certainly do not want to alleviate the blame from true criminals, you should understand that you are not a criminal for using mind control strategies.

Mind control in this day and age can be a powerful way to encourage people to do what you need or want them to do. Obviously, this type of powerful strategy can not only be used to have people do bad things or to create criminal results, but it can also be used to encourage positive results. Mind control is a technique whereby you use various psychological techniques to alter someone's mind. In doing so, you can change how they think about various things so that their thought processes work in your favor. This technique can enable you to achieve virtually anything you want with the help of virtually anyone you want. It truly puts you in the driver's seat of reality and allows you to have an effortless ability to live your desired life with your desired outcomes.

Brainwashing

Brainwashing is basically the procedure where somebody will be connived to abandon ideas that they had in the past in order to take new behavior and/or values. There is a great deal of manner in which this can be done, although not every one of them will certainly be considered bad. For example, if you are from an African nation and then relocate to America, you will usually be required to change your values and ideals in order to fit in with the new culture and environments you remain in. On the other hand, those in prisoner-of-war camps or when a brand-new totalitarian government is taking over will commonly undergo the process of indoctrination to persuade people to follow along in harmony.

Lots of people have misunderstandings of what brainwashing is. Some individuals have extra paranoid concepts concerning the technique consisting of mind control devices that are funded by the federal government and believed to be conveniently turned on like a push-button control. On the other side of points, there are skeptics that do not think that indoctrination is feasible in any way that any individual who asserts it has actually happened is lying. Generally, the practice of brainwashing will certainly land someplace in the center of these two concepts.

Throughout the practice of brainwashing, the subject will certainly be persuaded to transform their beliefs concerning something with a mix of different tactics. There is not just one method that can be utilized throughout this process, so it can be challenging to place the method right into a cool little box. Essentially, the topic will be divided from every one of the important things that they understand. From there, they will certainly be damaged down into an emotional state that makes them vulnerable before the new principles are presented. As the subject absorbs this brand-new detail, they will certainly be compensated for sharing ideas and ideas which support these new ideas. A reward will certainly be used to reinforce the brainwashing that is occurring. This is one of the most famous large scale CEM tactics. We hear about it happening in religions, cults, oppressive governments, and captive kidnapping victims. It is an intense form of social influence that can change someone's behavior and thoughts without their consent and often against their will.

Brainwashing requires the manipulator's total control over their victim, which is why it often requires total isolation of the victim such that their sleeping, eating, and basic needs are interrupted. The complete control required to brainwash someone is exactly the reason it occurs in cults and prison camps. In these settings, leaders have unfettered access to their vulnerable victims and can carry out their brainwashing techniques. In addition, those who join cults or are in prison camps are ideal candidates for brainwashing—they are vulnerable and are already prone to trying to find new ways of thinking because of their circumstances. Due to the victim's circumstantial flexibility of thought, brainwashing can take effect.

Who Uses Mind Control?

Media Producers

Just as our five senses are our guides in life, they can also be our enemies and traitors. Our sense of sight and the visual processing areas of the brain are very powerful. We almost always dream visually, even if another sense is missing, and we usually picture someone we are remembering rather than associating some other sensory input with them. This makes imagery and visual manipulation a particularly powerful technique of media mind control.

Traditionally, media production was in the hands of companies and institutions. These manipulative entities were able to pioneer the use of visual, subliminal mind control. Examples include split-second pictures of a product or person inserted into a seemingly innocent movie. Such split-second images, which the person perceives as nothing more than a flash of light, can take powerful control of a person's emotions. They have been used as recently as 21st-century Presidential elections.

Sound is another way in which a person is vulnerable to undetected mind control. Both experiments and personal experience will confirm this to you. Have you ever had a song stuck in your head? How easy was it to get rid of? The sound had a powerful influence over you, even though you knew it was present. The power of audio manipulation is even greater when it is undetected. Experiments have shown that if restaurant customers are exposed to music from a particular region, they are more likely to order wine from that country. When questioned, they had no idea that something as simple as sound had steered their decision.

Lovers

People are often a product of their environment, whether they want to be or not. The way people are raised directly affects the way they act in later life. People raised by alcoholics has a greater chance of becoming alcoholics in adult life, or they may choose never to drink. People raised in a house where everything is forbidden may cut loose and go a bit crazy when they are finally out on their own. People who are raised in total disorganization may grow up to be obsessive about household cleanliness.

Nurture affects people in other, less severe ways, too. Many people believe that Mom's meatloaf is the absolute best, and

no other recipe exists. People come from different religious and economic backgrounds and have different beliefs about what is good and bad, what is acceptable and unacceptable. The problem comes when two people try to have a relationship, but neither wants to change their way of thinking. When that happens, there is no relationship. There are just two people living together under the same roof. Achieving success in love is just like achieving success in anything else. It is mostly a function of developing good relationships with other people to be better able to influence them. Those people who are successful in creating and keeping good, mutually satisfactory relationships with others usually enjoy much more success than people who do not do this. The ability to grow and maintain satisfactory relationships is a trait that is easier for some people. But even if the ability does not come naturally, it is easy enough to learn. Neuro-Linguistic Programming (NLP) makes this skill easier to learn by offering tools and ideas to enable almost anyone to learn the ability to develop great relationships.
Salespeople

If a salesperson asks a regular customer to write a brief endorsement of the product they buy, hopefully, they will say yes. If someone asks their significant other to take some of the business cards to pass out at work, hopefully, they will say yes. If you write any kind of blog and ask another blogger to provide a link to yours on their blog, they will hopefully say yes. When enough people say yes, the business or blog will begin to grow. With even more yesses, it will continue to grow and thrive. This is the very simple basis of marketing. Marketing is nothing more than using mind control to get other people to buy something or to do something beneficial for someone else. And the techniques can easily be learned.

Writers

Think of writing a guest spot for someone else who has their blog. By sending in the entire manuscript first, there is a greater risk of rejection. Begin small. Send them a paragraph or two discussing the idea. Then outline the idea and send that in an email. Then write the complete draft you would like them to use and send it along. When asking a customer for a testimonial, start by asking for a few lines in an email. Then ask the customer to expand those few lines into a testimonial that covers at least half a typed page. Soon the customer will be ready for an hourlong webcast extolling the virtues of the product and your great customer service skills.

Everything must have a deadline that really exists. The important word here is the word 'real'. Everyone has heard the salesperson who said to decide quickly because the deal might not be available later or another customer was coming in, and they might get it. That is a total fabrication, and everyone knows it to be true. There are no impending other customers, and the deal is not going to disappear. There is no real sense of urgency involved. But everyone does it. There are too many situations where people are given a totally fake deadline by someone who thinks it will instill a great sense of urgency to complete the task. It is not only totally not effective but completely unneeded. It is a simple matter to create true urgency. Only leave free things available for a finite amount of time. When asking customers for testimonials, be certain to mention the last possible day for it to be received to be able to be used. Some people will be unable to assist, but having people unable to participate is better than never being able to begin.

In Education
By educating impressionable children, society essentially teaches them to become "ideal" members of society. They are taught and trained in certain ways that fulfill the government and authorities' desires, and most people don't even think twice about it.
Advertising and Propaganda

By putting advertising and propaganda everywhere, those in control can eliminate people's feeling of self-worth and encourage them to *need* what is being sold, as opposed to just wanting it. This is essentially a subliminal strategy to make people feel poorly about themselves to purchase whatever is being advertised to increase their feelings of self-worth.

Sports, Politics, Religion

The idea of these strategies is to "divide and conquer". Ultimately, each one has people placed into various categories, where they feel very strongly. As a result, they don't come together and support one another, but rather they are against each other. This means that they are divided, and so the authority can conquer.

Chapter 12 How to Analyze People Using Dark Psychology

In any kind of persuasion tactic, analyzing people is the key to hit or miss when it comes to success or failure. You can analyze a person by their word choice, behavior, vibes, body language, and even appearance. Each will be explained in detail in this chapter, together with examples and stories on how you can apply this knowledge yourself. Remember, even if a persuasion trick doesn't explicitly state to observe the person, you still should, as the best information you could obtain is through analysis. You can learn about a person's mood, some of their history, some personality traits, and even their attitude towards different situations simply by observing them. It's important to understand analysis, so absorb this information and take it with you to the final chapter, where you'll learn how to use all of these techniques for persuasion.

Word Choice

The words people chose to use in any given situation can tell a lot about them, such as their thoughts, feelings, and attitudes. A person's structure frames their written or spoken sentences are key indicators of what they thought or felt of the spoken event and even who they are as a person. If you pay attention to the chosen words that weren't necessary to form a correct sentence, you'll notice that there are a variety of options that person could have chosen. The fact that they deliberately opted for a certain word speaks volumes about who they are and what they think. For example, the sentence, "I worked on the paper," can be changed in various ways. All will still say that someone worked on a paper, however, each variation will tell you what they thought of the act and how well they performed it. If that person were to say, "I worked hard on the paper," the word 'hard' indicates that they take pride in the work they put in. This person strives for success and sets goals for themselves to achieve.

This paper was viewed by this person as a challenge that they took on and put great effort into overcoming. On the other hand, if someone states, instead, "I worked on the stupid paper," they show great resentment. Perhaps this is a student in a class they dislike, and they barely felt inclined to acknowledge the paper, let alone put any effort into it. This person is likely the type who would rather spend their time on something he/she enjoys and finds little value in work that doesn't immediately benefit them. Unlike the hard worker mentioned before, this person is laxer in their work ethic and succeeds in other life areas than academics.

Different statements create different meanings. Simple statements such as, "I earned an award" suggest that this person believes success is earned and not given, versus the common statement, "I won an award". You can learn a lot about a person by listening to what they choose to say. For example, when I was still in my high school years, I observed a young girl barely younger than I was at the time. She was discussing about a teacher with a small group of students. The trio was very loud with their declarations, which indicated that they didn't mind the possibility of others hearing them, nor did they worry such opinions may come back around on them. The girl stood with defiance in her body language, something that will be discussed later on, and she held her head high. She said, "Mr. Borrock is a moron. I don't know who gave him a teaching degree, but he doesn't know what he's talking about!" To which the girl standing directly across from her snickered and replied, "I know. I transferred to Ms. Ally's class because she's a lot better. She doesn't even grade the homework! If you turn it in, you get an A. Much better than Borrock."

Of course, I changed the names for security reasons, but the statements themselves are what is important. Using only the first girl's statement, you can imagine that she values her own opinion above that of others. She deliberately uses demeaning language when describing her teacher and even denounces his teaching credibility. By stating that Mr. Borrock "Doesn't know what he's talking about," she insinuates that she learns nothing from his teachings. This statement points to arrogance and a lack of respect for authority. The second girl eagerly agrees with the first, but her opinion on the situation is greatly different. She boasts that Ms. Ally is a better teacher, but this statement isn't backed up by her teaching method and how much she is learning in her class. She prefers this teacher that is more casual in her grading strategy. These words indicate that she takes minimal pride in her education and finds little to no learning value. Because this conversation stems from the group of students feeding off of each other's comments, they all are gregarious in nature and feel more comfortable and confident to reveal their opinions in a group. There are many other ways to read word choices and phrases people choose to use. Always watch for the difference between phrases like "I like him, and I'm fond of him," as 'like' is a very general word that can vary in meaning. Often it is used as a placement word for a lack of real emotion. If you like something, you may range from tolerating it to enjoying it. Without a real indication, however, it usually indicates the former. Fondness, however, is a true emotion. If you are fond of someone, you enjoy being around them. Other differences are, "I bought you a gift," and "I bought you another gift," as the word 'another' indicates resentment or strongly hints at the need for gratitude. This is a strong display of a person in need of power. By learning people's words, you will be learning them.

Body Language

Many professions require the need to learn general body language. Agents in the criminal justice field must know the difference between someone innocent's behavior and that of a criminal. Psychiatrists must know how their sessions make their client feel, so they must know the difference between a person with their head down and their eyes hidden and someone who is making eye contact openly. Whatever the reason, the study of body language isn't uncommon. Even so, it is important when you are trying to persuade someone. If a person is rigid and looking down, it isn't a good moment to ask something of them, as they are guarded, and their mind is elsewhere. If they are looking at you with relaxed shoulders and their body is facing you, however, they trust you and are genuinely interested in what you are saying. This is a preferable moment to ask a favor than the previous example. If someone is sitting across from you, you can tell their opinion of you based solely on how they are sitting.
For example, if their arms are crossed, they are feeling uncomfortable. If they lean away from you, they don't care much for your presence. Whether or not someone consistently looks at you is always a huge indicator, as eye contact is important for a conversation in many countries. If this person is covering their hands somehow, be it stuffing them in their pockets, holding them in their lap under the table, or folding them behind their backs, it usually means they are hiding something. If a person is picking at their cuticles or nails, biting their lips or nails, or fidgeting in their seat, they are

displaying discomfort. This can be created from a lie, nervousness in an awkward situation, or a difficult conversation topic.

For example, if you have a casual conversation with someone, and they are leaning towards you slightly and looking at your face, they are interested and engaged in the conversation. However, if you ask a personal matter that this person would rather not speak about, he or she may scratch the back of their neck, bite their lip, or run his or her thumb along their other hand. They might also look down, and their shoulders will hunch forward in a manner that is considered curling into themselves. These signs indicate that the subject is uncomfortable and possibly off limits at that time. Unless they state they would like to continue, it is best to steer the subject to a safer place until the relationship builds more. If someone feels their privacy is invaded, they will block you out and you will need to redevelop the rapport you had built.

Behavior

A person or animal's behavior tells you a lot about them. In the wild, experts observe certain behaviors to study them and better understand the wild animal and its way of life. A wildlife specialist may observe how cheetah cubs fight each other and will explain that they are playing in a productive way for survival, as they are training to fight and hunt. An adult lion will often pretend to be harmed as their child playfully attacks them to promote hunter instinct and ability. A runt of a litter may be excluded from the family in certain activities, as it is a liability and the weakest link. These same observations may be turned towards humans as well. An example is the common feuding of siblings. As the older sibling, I personally feel that, as a general rule, younger siblings can be spotted a mile away. They tend to make their complaints heard more loudly than older siblings, and they grow up to be much more competitive.

A person born as the youngest sibling may also be laxer in their ethics and drive to be productive, as parents usually aren't as strict in their discipline by the time the younger children are born. However, I have met many people who swear that they know what an older sibling looks like. I've been told we older siblings act like the parent to everyone around us, as we were the family's born babysitters. I've also been told that we tend to need control with the resentment toward the lax parenting of the younger siblings. I personally don't see it, which is an obvious sign that it must apply to me as well.

Other than birth order, you can also learn desires from behaviors. I once walked around the mall with a couple of friends of mine. Both were female. Upon passing a store filled with cartoon and videogame characters, all three of us ran through the door and nearly squealed at every object with a character we like displayed on it. My shortest friend insisted on buying friendship charms that produced obvious excitement from all of us. A month later, I walked past that same store with a male friend whose interests couldn't differ more than my female companions. Not wanting to appear childish, I purposely did not look at that store or make a comment about it. Had he been paying attention, my friend would have noticed my straighter shoulders and back, my folded hands, and my sudden lack of interest in my surroundings. Being a curious person by nature, I often look around me. My desire that could have been noticed at that time was to hide something about myself from my friend. Because behaviors develop over time, they tend to indicate deeper information about a person than the other analysis techniques. You'll know what really makes this person tick if you observe enough of them.

Vibes

There's always going to be debate on whether or not "vibes" exist and what they really are. Many deny them as a made-up concept of those same magic users who manipulate people with their cold reading. Others brush it off as nonsense that people choose to believe in. The universal truth, however, is that people give off a feeling when you are around them. Whatever you want to call it, it is there. Some people give off vibes that make you feel happier and generally better than before you were around them. Those people tend to have many others flock around them because the feeling is infectious. These people are often gregarious and smile often. On the other hand, other people are known in more spiritual communities as "Energy Vampires". These people's presences tend to "suck" the feeling away from the rest. They tend to carry a dark mood with them and often hold their heads down and even speak with negative intent. An Energy Vampire may frequently make side remarks such as "She's such a suck-up" regarding a friendlier person asking another if they require assistance. It's important to learn what your vibes are so you know how approachable you are and whether or not you exude that feeling of positivity that draws people in.

Appearance

Strangely enough, appearance can tell you a lot about someone. Though the phrase "don't judge a book by its cover" has circulated through everyone's mind since childhood, you really can learn a lot about that book simply by looking over the cover. If you see a man sitting at a coffee shop wearing a neatly pressed suit with his hair combed neatly atop his head, you can safely assume that he is a man who cares about the opinions of those around him. Unless he's waiting patiently for another man for a meeting, he has no obligation to dress as he does. People who take this much care in their appearance usually also stand with a high posture and give value and pride in their work. They may also thrive on high praise when it comes to their careers and follow social rules such as arriving early, practicing diligence, and always remaining patient. This is one of the main reasons why it is a known rule to dress professionally for any kind of job interview, regardless of the dress code once you're hired. On the other hand, a person who dresses more casually puts comfort above outside appearance. This person may care only for personal comforts or pleasures when all other duties have been taken care of, or no immediate responsibilities are taking his or her time. Though this person may put effort into their work, they tend to take their time and won't frequently prioritize work above all else. This person may often be late to events or become distracted often.

Of course, it is unwise to make deductions about someone based on their appearance alone. It is simply a tool you can combine with the other methods described in this chapter. For example, say a woman is at a grocery store wearing a simple, stained shirt, and sweatpants and her hair is thrown out of the way without a care as to what it looks like. She is pushing a cart full of baby diapers, children's toys, ingredients to make a meal, and exhaustion is written all over her face. By clothing alone, she might appear lazy and uncaring. However, if you consider the child products of different ages and groceries, it is safe to assume she is pressed for time and resources. Appearance just isn't high on her priorities.

On the other hand, if this same woman was standing in an aisle without any urgency, buying little, visibly nervous, and giving off the vibes associated with an Energy Vampire, that might be a different story.

You may choose to judge a book by its cover; however, it is important to test a couple of pages and the description to make certain before deciding whether or not to buy it.

Chapter 13 Tactics to Manipulate Others

Everyone in the world has likely used manipulation at some point in their lives. This could have been through telling the most straightforward lies to get out of situations or flirting with others to get what you want. In understanding the techniques used by manipulators in their work, you need to ask yourself the following question:

Who is threatened by a manipulator? To regulate their victims, the pullers of the strings (manipulators) use several tactics, but most importantly, they do this by targeting specific kinds of personalities. You are more likely to be a victim of manipulation if you have low self-esteem, if you are inexperienced, easily pleased, if you are not confident about yourself and if you lack assertive instincts.

What are the requirements for successful manipulation?

Primarily, successful manipulation encompasses a manipulator. Manipulation is also likely to be achieved through covert hostile methods. For successful persuasion, a manipulator has to:

- **Cover their violent purposes, deeds, and be friendly.**

- **Be aware of the targeted person's psychological susceptibilities to conclude which strategies are likely to be the most effective.**

- **Have an adequate level of callousness to have no doubts about triggering injury to the victim if necessary.**

The manipulators exploit different defenselessness habits that exist in the victim's character and such include:

- **The naïveté of the targeted person** - Based on naïveté, the targeted person experiences hardships to buy the notion that many human beings are always sneaky, deceitful, and hard-nosed. This means if you are the victim, you will be in denial that you are being victimized.

- **If you are over-conscientiousness** - This is where you find yourself ready to grant the exploiter the advantage of distrust. The manipulator ends up blaming you and supporting their side, which makes you trust them easily. If you are too honest, you end up thinking everyone else is reliable as well.

- **Self-confidence** - Controllers often check whether you are a self-doubting person and whether you lack self-assertiveness, which makes you go into a defensive mode effortlessly. You end up not giving a second thought about errors.

- **Over-intellectualization** - This makes it hard for you to understand and therefore you end up believing your manipulator's reasons for being hurtful.

- **Your emotional reliance** - If you have a submissive personality, you are more likely to be a victim of manipulation. The more you rely on your emotions, the more vulnerable you are to being manipulated.

- **Loneliness** - If you are a lonely person, you are likely to agree to take little social interaction proposals. Some manipulators will propose being your companion, but at a price. This also involves being narcissistic so you fall easily for any kind of unjustified flattery. Lonely people act without any consultations. Therefore, loneliness goes hand in hand with being impulsive.

- **Materialistic** - Having a get-rich-quick mindset makes you cheap prey for manipulators. This means you are greedy and want to get rich quickly, so you

end up acting immorally for some sort of material exchange.

- **The elderly are also at a higher risk of getting controlled easily because they are fatigued and unable to multitask.** Likelihoods the elderly will have a thought that a manipulator might be a conman are very rare. Manipulators thus take advantage of them and commit elder abuse.

Techniques of Manipulation

Manipulators take time to explore and examine your characteristics and find out how vulnerable you are to exploitation. They tend to control their victims by playing with their psychological characters. Having read the points above, you should now know what tactics and techniques are manipulators use to control their victims. They include various methods, as discussed below.

Reinforcement: This can be either positive, negative, or intermittent forms of reinforcement.

- **Positive reinforcement:** This involves the case where the manipulator uses praises, charms, crocodile tears, unnecessary apologizing, public acknowledgment, cash, presents, consideration, and facial language like forced laughter or smiles.

- **Negative reinforcement:** A manipulator removes you from a negative situation as a favor.

- **Intermittent reinforcement:** This is also known as partial reinforcement. This creates an environment full of fear and doubts. It encourages the victim of manipulation to persist.

Punishment: The manipulator acts in a nagging manner. There is yelling, silent treatment, intimidating behavior, and threatening of the victim. Manipulators cry and tend to play the victim card, thus emotionally blackmailing the victim and can go further by swearing they are the innocent one. **Lying**: it entails two ways; lying by commission and lying by omission.

1. **Lying by commission** - You will find it hard to tell when a manipulator is lying at the moment they do it, and the truth won't be revealed until it is too late. You should understand that some people are experts at lying and, therefore, you should not give in easily to their tactics.

2. **Lying by omission** - This is a subtle way used to manipulate, and it entails telling lies, and at the same time, withholding significant amounts of the facts. It is also applied in propaganda.

Denial: Manipulators rarely admit they are wrong. Even when they have done something wrong, they will refuse to believe it. They are rational and always assert that their behavior is not harmful or that they are not as bad as someone else has explained. They accompany every exploitation with phrases like, 'it was only a joke'.

Attention: This includes selective inattention and attention. In this case, manipulators deliberately refuse to listen or pay attention to anything that distracts them from their agendas. They always defend themselves with phrases like, 'I do not need to listen to that'.

Deviation: Controllers never answer any questions directly and always steer the discussion to another topic. If not so, the manipulator gives irrelevant or rogue answers to the direct questions asked.

Intimidation: In this case, the manipulator applies two methods of intimidation; covert intimidation and guilt trip. In underground extortion, the manipulators throw their targets onto the self-justifying side through the use of implied threats. A guilt trip is a technique where the manipulator tries to suggest to the meticulous prey that they no longer care, and this makes the victim feel bad, and they start doubting

themselves, so they find themselves in a submissive position.
Use of Sarcasm: The manipulator shames the victim by using put-downs and sarcasm that makes the victim doubt. Making the victim feel unworthy gives an entry for the manipulator to defer the victim. These shaming tactics may include fierce glances, unpleasant tones, rhetorical comments or questions, and subtle sarcasm. Some of the victims end up not daring to challenge the manipulator as it fosters a sagacity of meagerness to their targets.
Belittling their Target: Manipulators use this technique to put their target on the self-justifying side while at the same time covering the belligerent aims of the persuader. The persuader then misleadingly blames their target in response to the victim's defensive mechanisms. This also involves the case where a manipulator plays the victim role by portraying themselves as victims of circumstances to gain sympathy, and thereby, getting what they want. This technique aims at caring and compassionate victims as some people cannot stand seeing someone suffer, and thus, the manipulator takes that chance to get the victim's cooperation.
Feigning: The manipulator pretends that any harm caused was unintentional or they are being accused falsely. Manipulators often wear a surprised face, hence making the victim question their sanity. Feigning also involves the case where the manipulator plays dumb and pretends to be totally unaware of what the victim is talking about. The victim starts doubting themselves while the manipulator continues to point out the main ideas they included, just in case there is any doubt. This happens only if the manipulator had used cohorts in advance to help back up their stories.
Seduction: In this case, the manipulator uses praise or any form of flattery, which involves supporting the victim to gain their conviction. Manipulators can even start helping you to increase your loyalty, and it will be hard for you to suspect

their evil intentions. The manipulator can also play the servant role where their actions will be justified by phrases such as, 'I am just doing my job' or 'I am in service to a certain authority figure.' In this case, the victim will give their trust and end up being manipulated.

Brandishing anger: The manipulator shows how angry they are to intensify the victim's shock to get their submission. In the real sense, the manipulator is never angry, but they act like they are, especially when denied access to what they want. A manipulator can as well control their anger to avoid any confrontations or hide their intentions. Manipulators often threaten the victims by saying they are going to report the cases to the police. Anger is a way of blackmailing the victim into not telling the truth, as it wards off any further inquiries. This makes the victim focus more on the manipulator's anger than on the manipulation technique being used.

The bandwagon effect: This is the case where the manipulator tends to comfort the victim by claiming that, whether right or wrong, many people have already done some things, and thus, the victim should do it anyway. The manipulator uses phrases like 'Many people like you...' This kind of manipulation is mainly applied to those under peer pressure conditions. Similar cases are when a manipulator tries to lure the victim into taking drugs or abusing other substances. The techniques discussed above are the tested and proven tactics that any manipulator will strive to use to get a strong control of their victims. Before a manipulator persuades their victims, there are those steps they have to follow to make sure they fully control their victim's minds. Whatever the reasons for manipulating someone, you should always play your cards safely. That is why you should learn how to manage and control people's thoughts, the strategies, and steps you need to use in various situations. There are three authentic manipulating skills you can learn quickly through the steps discussed below. If you want to manipulate others easily, come on! Shed a fake tear and follow the following steps.

Apply Different Persuasion and Manipulation Techniques

Always start with unreasonable requests to get more reasonable ones: This step is a time-tested persuasion technique. As a manipulator, you should always start with unreasonable demands and then wait for the victim to deny you, then follow it up with a more approachable request. It will be hard for them to reject you for the second time, as the second request will sound more appealing than the first request.

Ask for a rare request before YOUR real request: This is another way of getting what you want as it entails requesting a strange thing that throws your target off guard, making them unable to deny you. Then ask for the more usual type of request, and the victim will not be able to deny it since their mind has been trained to avoid these activities.

Stimulate fear, then liberation: For successful persuasion, tell the person what they fear, and then relieve them of it, and with no doubt, they will be happy to grant your wish. It may sound mean, but you will get your results instantly.

Make your target feel guilty: Making your target feel guilty is another step for successful manipulation. You need to start by picking someone susceptible to feeling guilty. This should be followed by making them feel like they are bad for not granting your requests, no matter how absurd it is. The following can be the unchallenging victims who will fall into your persuasion technique:

- Parents - Manipulate your parents by making them feel guilty. Mention to them how you feel your life is full of suffering since childhood because they are not granting your wishes.

- Friends - Remind them of all the good deeds you have done for them or tell them how they usually let you down.

- Significant partner - Conclude your quarrels by saying, 'Okay- I expected this.' This will make them feel guilty about letting you down several times.

Bribe: In this step, blackmailing is not necessary to get your wishes granted. Bribe your victim with an unappealing present. You can as well offer something you would have done anyway. First, you should figure out what your targeted person wants or lacks at the moment, then try giving it to them. Secondly, do not make it sound like you are bribing, but portray yourself like someone who is willing to help your victim in return for something you want.

Playing the Victim: Making yourself the victim is always a great manipulation technique. You should use this step sparingly and effectively to pierce your victim's heart and get what you want. You have to act like you are a wonderful person, philanthropic, and that you are always the victim of every evil on earth. Play dumb as it makes your victim believe you are honestly perplexed by why evil things always befall you. Saying 'It is okay- I'm used to this' makes your victim feel like someone who cannot avoid helping you several times, and this tactic will make you get what you want. Finally, always be pathetic.
'It is okay- I'm used to this'

Apply logic: This step works better for rational-minded people. Logic acts as the most excellent persuader, more so when you carry along with come-oriented whys and wherefores on how what you are after would benefit both of you. While presenting your case, do it calmly and rationally to avoid losing your control. If you want to manipulate a rational person, NEVER be emotional. In this step, act like your request is the only option you have, and your victim will judge the case your way.

Never Break Character: When your friend, family member, or co-worker tries to manipulate you, pretend to be more upset than them. Look more hurt and tell them you are even amazed and you did not believe they could ever think that about you.

This will make the victim feel guilty and sorry for you.

Chapter 14 How to Understand and Connect With Other People's Emotions

Humans are emotion-driven, irrational monsters of the natural world. Despite our best wishes, emotions and feelings drive our actions far more than logic and reason. That's okay most of the time because they often indicate an appropriate course of action.

But then there are times when our emotions betray us or at least serve our goals poorly. Without training to identify and overcome the natural cognitive bias we all hold, our emotions open us up to most of the techniques covered so far. Even people trained to identify and overcome the irrational parts of the brain struggle to resist. These individuals appear resistant but are as weak to social manipulation as anyone else. They just require a more adept and skilled hand.

We can't have a conversation about social manipulation without talking about Stanley Milgram and his experiments. That's because the techniques Mr. Milgram used are brutally effective and repeatable. They also have terrifying implications about authority and acts of evil. Primary Question: How far will someone go to obey an authority figure, even when ordered to act against their moral conscience?

Methods: Volunteers were asked to "teach" other people to improve their ability to remember. A man in a white coat posing as a doctor asked the volunteer teacher to administer questions to a "learner" in another room within earshot. If the learner answered incorrectly, the teacher was directed to provide an electric shock.

The idea was that for every wrong answer, the shock would teach them not to answer incorrectly. After every mistake, the doctor directed the teacher to increase the voltage delivered to the learner. The control panel presented to the teacher included settings in 10-volt increments up to a lethal 450 volts.

If a teacher protested and asked to stop, the doctor would reply, "The experiment must go on." Any protests or questions from the teachers would be answered with the same words. The doctors were not otherwise allowed to coerce and were strictly forbidden from forcing them to do anything. An actor played the learner in the other room and screamed, wailed, pleaded, and begged the teacher to stop before finally going silent. It's important that the teacher not see the learner during the experiment or the success rate drops. The learners can scream and plea all they want.

Results: In one example, about 90% of teachers delivered a lethal shock before stopping. Only about 1% of the population was willing to go all the way to the maximum shock without coercion. But despite teachers voicing protests to the doctor, they continued to conduct the test. Often teachers continued to deliver fatal shocks long after the learner stopped replying to prompts.

Even though having a form of authority is a major contributor to success in social manipulation, it's not foolproof. You have to leverage that authority properly to produce the best results. There are twelve strategies to accomplish this task in a minimum amount of time.

Fear is one of the most powerful emotions. It captures our attention like nothing else, threatening everything we hold dear.

It forces us to focus on it and shuts down our higher thinking.

It doesn't matter that violence is on a global centuries-long decline. It's easy to manufacture situations that make it seem like extreme violence is the norm. Just hone in on the frightening but statistical rarities.

Terrorist attacks and mass shootings might be rare compared to lightning strikes and police killings, but are terrifying enough to shut down our creative thinking skills and force us to focus on defending ourselves. This fear is then easily translated into fear at whatever scapegoat is convenient.

Example: Major news networks understand the power of fear. They offer 24-hour coverage of all the things going wrong in the world. They offer a warped view because they prioritize content that produces a strong emotional reaction to an accurate representation of the facts.

Many creatures naturally respond to fear with anger and aggression. When you are a mouse cornered by a cat, it makes sense to go on the offensive. In such situations, the risk of dying is outweighed by the chance of escape. This dichotomy is often referred to as the fight or flight response.

There are tons of times when our fear is justified, but we can set up false dichotomies in our every-day life that make us feel like a trapped mouse when we really aren't. Mass media makes its bread and butter off setting up and playing up any threat they can.

The bigger and more complex the issue, the more anger and hostility it generates. Offering a simple solution might never fix the problem, but most people prefer doing something, even if it makes things worse. If it does exacerbate the situation, it is easy to blame the increased tension on the complex and intractable problem.

Example: Provoking hostility and rage is a simple matter when you know what people are afraid of. That's why politicians are so good at stoking up fervor in their supporters.

They identify the fears of their constituents, blame scapegoats, and offer simple answers to intractable solutions. There have been many people who claimed to be the only person can do what needs to be done. These people are almost always dominant and strong-willed. They offer domination and don't think twice about making unrealistic claims. The best way to become a messiah is by leveraging the afterlife. However, this does not always involve religion. Many dictators present themselves as the only person capable of bringing back a mythical golden age.

This strategy leverages nostalgia and totalitarian security to alleviate a social fear. It relies on the promise of better things to come to justify whatever the Great Leader desires. This makes it more effective with conservative populations than liberal ones.

Example: To gain control over a group, I would claim to be the only person who can "Make Things Great Again." I position myself as the sole authority willing to do what needs to be done. This forces anyone in the group to remain silent on issues they might disagree on. The silence acts as a form of de facto consent, which prevents others from speaking out for fear of being the only one to go against the Great Leader. The world is supremely complex and there are many ways to accomplish any given goal. But this idea doesn't make people feel very secure, so we tend to simplify things.

Simplifying complex problems normally isn't an issue. But when all possible responses are reduced to two options, it can set up a false and misleading dilemma. This warped view of things makes it easy to justify all sorts of bad behavior. Reducing the world to black-and-white narratives appeals to our desire for simple and clean resolutions to complex and messy problems. It becomes more effective when we are on the brink of catastrophe. When people are afraid and angry, they often accept these oversimplifications and alluring but empty promises.

Social - Being Liked

Sociality has a huge impact on how easily people are influenced. Social proof means how well we are accepted by people and groups, whether personal or professional. We are influenced in social situations through three main factors - authority, likability, and social proof. We are influenced by authority figures, by the people we like and those who provide us with social proof. For instance, a teenager at school would gain 'social proof' if seen mingling with the popular crowd. Since humans are social creatures, we want to feel connected to one another and as though we're part of something bigger. For this reason, we're more likely to do something simply because we see others doing it. For instance, in a sales negotiation, a company may show a potential new client all the other businesses in the area they deal with. Or in a one-toone situation we can influence someone by explaining Mr. Popular from another department agreed to it. Knowing others have taken some action before us helps to naturally reduce resistance.

Authority

We're naturally more influenced by those we deem to be above us in some respect. You're more likely to follow directions when they come from management at your place of work rather than if they came from a fellow colleague. We look up too and respect those who are an expert within a certain area or subject, we see these people as an authority. Something as simple as informing an audience or an individual of your credentials before an interaction can help swing the odds into your favor when looking to persuade or influence. This technique can also be effective when emailing, as simply stating at the beginning about any skills you possess in relation to the subject can help make the other person more susceptible to your influence. For example, if you were contacting someone about the possibility of speaking at their event and you had previous experience of speaking at big events, the mere mention of the biggest events you've spoken at would have an impact on the way the recipient would view your application. We can use this to our advantage and maybe even exaggerate our accomplishments.

Consistency

This is another means of getting people to buy-in to us and is often used as a sales tactic. In this method we ask the target to admit their goals and priorities first and then align our request with their desires. This makes it difficult for them to say no too. Use the information they originally provided and offer them a solution based upon it.

People like to remain consistent and don't like being seen as dishonest, so it makes it harder for them to reject a request that matches their needs. When a target shares their goals first, they are invested, once they're invested, we can offer them the right solutions.

Here are a few further strategies can be used to influence.

This method is named Disrupt and Reframe - This process involves mixing up the words, behaviors, or visuals a person is used to and then reframing our pitch/request while they're

still trying to figure out the disruption. This method was put to the test by researchers who sold a product giving customers two different options.
The first choice offered $3 for 8 apples

The second option offered 300 cents for 8 apples

The second choice was the clear winner, selling almost twice as many apples as option 1.
This technique works because the target has less resistance to the reframe (option 2) as the brain is thrown off by the initial disruption of the unusual wording.

Storytelling

Another method of getting people onside is through storytelling. This enables others to identify with us and the various aspects of our story, which helps build trust. However, it is important our story contains the right plot. The three main plots for an influential story are -
 1. *Challenge Plot* - This is the underdog story, the rags to riches, the person who made it through some adversity on sheer willpower.

 2. *Connection Plot* - Another common plot, where people build a relationship that bridges a certain gap.
    This can be racial, cultural, class, ethnic etc.

 3. *Creative Plot* - This is a story where someone achieves a breakthrough of some sort. Whether

solving a long-lasting problem or overcoming an issue in a brand new or innovative way.

If you have any personal stories that can make you meet any of the above criteria, you should find it easier to hook people in.

Paradoxical Intervention

This term is simply another way of saying 'Reverse Psychology'. This is a term most of us are familiar with and has been used for years.
Reverse psychology is a persuasion method that many of us tend to use unconsciously. It involves getting someone to do something we want by suggesting the opposite. This tactic tends to work better when our target is stressed and is making emotional decisions instead of thinking things through.
A simple form of reverse psychology is telling someone 'not to do X', by suggesting this we are implanting this very idea into their mind. As we know, children naturally want to do whatever they've been forbidden to do. We can take this further also. If someone commits to something, we can ensure they follow through by expressing doubt over what they have promised. This will make them assert themselves by completing the action in a bid to prove us wrong.

Examples of Reverse Psychology

Here are some basic examples of where we may come across reverse psychology in our day to day life.

A mother suggests to her stingy teenager son that he can't afford to buy his sister a birthday gift. The boy reacts to this by buying his sister an expensive present.

An office worker who is fed up with a lazy colleague who doesn't pull his weight. May say 'Ok, don't help me. I don't care'. This prompts the colleague to help out.

Or the shy boy who reacts to his friends, who suggest he's not interested in girls, by asking a girl out as his prom date.

Reverse psychology is more likely to be effective with those who desire control, such as rebellious teenagers or type A personalities. They feel that by going against others, they're in control. But we can expose this vulnerability for our gain. When someone suggests that reverse psychology is being used deliberately. Then reversing the reverse can help. It certainly helps if we act indifferent to whatever decision is made. One problem with reverse psychology is that if there are other options or alternatives to what we have suggested, the person might choose something else altogether.

Chapter 15 Deception

The average person tells several lies every day. We are trained to lie to protect ourselves. We lie to protect others. We lie to ourselves, not even being aware of it. Just because it is extremely prevalent doesn't mean it isn't a great tool for manipulation. For example, how many white lies do parents tell their children to protect their innocence or just to make them easier to deal with at the moment. Now, these white lies may be to protect them, but it is to control them for their benefit. Most people can agree that lying to kids protects their innocence and is worth it, right?

The key is not to become a pathological liar, only lie when you have something to gain and a bulletproof story to back you up as well. You must nail down the details before ever repeating it to avoid mistakes. If you don't have time to plan out your lie effectively, telling the truth, even if it is a truth you don't approve of, is almost always going to be the better choice.

You can create an effective lie in several ways. You can leave details out of a true story to mislead a person, emphasizing what you want them to hear. The key is that they believe you. You cannot mislead someone who does not believe what you are saying. Remember that the truth is actually based on a person's perception of what matters to them and what they have already learned. Your job is to challenge that.

The truth is you are surrounded by deceitful people. You will look at their social media posts and see pictures of how much fun they are having and how happy their family looks, when actually, the pictures are orchestrated, and the family barely speaks to each other. Have you ever had a friend who was cheated on and acted like it is no big deal? Odds are they were actually devastated and may have even stopped believing in love. Now their life is just a show. Push play and go. Lies come in many forms. Your lies form a foundation for you to analyze a person on a deeper level, telling them whatever they want or need to hear. You should be observing and leading your subject.

During your job interview, didn't your potential employer talk about the company's values and goals, making it seem like you would be lucky to work there? In reality, they have no values, they don't give a crap about their employees, and you just found out that they lost half the staff in one year. Think back to the interview, how nervous you were, wondering if you would be chosen. They were lying to you, and you did not care because of your personal goals at the time.

You might not even realize how much the people in your life have lied to you. At first you might think that this would be a horrible thing. However, the reason people lie varies and should not be taken personally. We think we know what is best for our loved ones, but sometimes they might surprise you, and the reasons might surprise you even more. This is why I encourage you to be deceitful to achieve what you want, because at the end of the day if you do not take control of your own life, someone else could be doing it for you. This is where your story is either a truth or a lie, a mix of both, depending on what you need someone to believe about you. Do not let others dictate your life by the stories they tell about you, especially to other people, you have to enforce your story by emphasizing what you want to be remembered for.

Starting Your Deception

Now it is your turn to enjoy lying, to master the universe with your narrative. You will create the world you want in your mind, and one lie at a time, make that world a reality. The first important lie is that you care. You will have to work on your empathy. With all the other tools in this book, you should be on a good starting path to understanding how to read people. Empathy is a view taken on from your subject's perspective. You want to walk in their shoes. This gives you the window to know what it is that they really want to hear. You are trying to know what they know. Take an interest in your subject's hobbies or work. This display of interest is a path to telling them what you want them to think, but in the context of what excites them. Try making a comparison to keep the momentum going.

Be sure that when setting your goal for your lie, you also set the stage. Start by examining your social media posts. Start posting things that interest your subject. They are likely to start to follow your posts. Update your profile. Get dressed up and ask a stranger to take a picture of you at the coffee shop. It will look like a friend took it and you are out having fun. Put on a flattering outfit, make sure it is still your style and check in somewhere trendy.

Find a cause that you can appear passionate about, but that is not too controversial. This will give you credit for being viewed as a compassionate person. People will respect that you believe in something, and it will help you appear to have depth as a person. Another way of making someone believe that you care about what they are saying is to ask many questions to analyze what their interests are. You can achieve this by asking about the types of books they like to read or what is their favorite city in the US. Have a few follow-up questions ready.

Tell Your Own Story

Write down what you want to be remembered for. Do you want to be known as a rich person, defined by money? Tell that story.

Do you want to be remembered for being charitable? Tell that story. Do you want to be memorable in the first place? It is important to be sure to tell your stories with care. I am going to tell you a story about my rich Aunt Betty. Aunt Betty made a lot of money suing people and writing stories for the gossip magazines of the 1990s. She put her money in the bank and a trust. She made me trustee, and I did not even know it. No one knew Aunt Betty had money. She drove a 15-year-old car. She never wore any jewelry. She drank cheap wine. She would complain about how expensive everything had become. She sold her house and moved into a small apartment after her seventieth birthday.

I thought my aunt was one of the happiest people I knew. She did not worry about too much, citing that it was out of her hands. She never had any of her kids, but she took her nieces and nephews to Disneyland every year. All the other family members thought she starved all year to afford that trip. We just went along with everything until one day she died. My mother told me she did not have anything valuable and a lawyer was taking care of her last bit of business she left behind. One night after work, I got a call from Aunt Betty's lawyer about her trust. I was in shock. Aunt Betty had a trust? This lawyer said he wasn't that far from my house and wanted me to sign the acceptance papers, which had a secrecy clause. Aunt Betty had trusted me with her secret. She had a boatload of money, over a million dollars. To wrap this story up, she left it all to a charity. She paid me to make sure that the lawyer gave all the money to the charity. But I could never tell a soul how she deceived all of us. I admired her so much for being a con, I kept her secret. Besides, she paid me well.

At first, hearing about my Aunt Betty's trust, I felt bad for my mom and her siblings because they had no idea who their sister was. They thought she was a poor old woman who complained a lot. But instead, she was a generous person who believed that she should have money for a rainy day. She hated the thought of asking anyone for help. She wanted her leftover money to go to helping people. She believed her family could help themselves and that they would fight over money. She lied to them about her success, not outright, but in the form of a secret. In the end, a wonderful charity received money that would reach many needy people. That helped Aunt Betty sleep at night. Whatever your life goals are, you have to be willing to protect them, and deception might be the only way to keep others from sabotaging you. People are so wrapped up in themselves that they will not even notice that you are not an open book, posting everything about yourself for the world to see. When you get questioned about your life, you will read the script that you wrote. You decide who you are, no one else. It is a good idea to have a few stories rehearsed. Rehearsing out loud is encouraged so you can hear the tone, and it will increase your chances of memorizing the stories. My personal favorite way to pull up a story to be able to relate to a person is to live vicariously through another person's story, making absolutely sure that the person you are telling the story to does not know the person who you stole the story from.

The point is that sometimes the truth does not serve you or your goals. Once you feel comfortable with this idea, things will get a lot easier for you. People do not need to know everything about us, just to be able to use it against us later. You will be smarter than that. Let your target fall for that and reveal themselves for you to influence. That is why I say; the world is yours because you can literally transform it. Get to work on writing your "script."

Tips for Lying Effectively

Crank up the empathy: Before you start bending the truth for your benefit, you must already form an emotional bond with the other party, as this will make them far more likely to believe you. This means you need to come on strong, right from the beginning, as it typically only takes about two minutes for a person to decide if they like someone they have just met. If you fall on the wrong side of this initial appraisal, then you are going to have a much more difficult time convincing them of anything, even the truth. As such, you will need to watch any new target you are considering beforehand to get the clearest picture of their personality type as possible. Once you have a general idea of how they think and act, you can then introduce a version of yourself that matches their expectations, making anything else you need to do far more manageable as a result.

Know common tells: Most people get caught when they lie is because they telegraph their actions without even realizing it. If you hope to ever deceive others effectively, you will need to learn then, so you can learn to avoid using them. The most common signs that show someone is lying include odd hand gestures, looking away from the person target of the conversation, speaking too quickly and pausing before speaking. If you can remove these from your behaviors while telling a lie, then there will be less of a gap between the question and the answer and less of a reason for the person you are speaking with not to trust you.

Watch your body language: When a person tells a lie, they commonly adopt a defensive, closed posture. As such, a great way to assure the other party that you are not lying is to adopt open body language instead. This includes things like standing with your arms casually at your sides, which says you are open to the conversation that you are a part of and are anxious to reach a consensus. You will also want to ensure that you stand facing them and slowly move closer to them as you continue the conversation. Finally, you must ensure you don't place anything that could be considered a barrier between you, even if it is just a file folder.

Your hands are also very important, especially when you are interacting with someone new. Studies show that gesturing with your hands makes other people more likely to believe whatever you are saying. Likewise, a firm, non-aggressive handshake is important for getting off on the right foot in anything other than a causal relationship.

Conclusion

This book set aside some effort to investigate the diverse manipulation systems that are available on the planet today, just as a portion of the strategies and methods that accompany every sort. Each of the mind control methods works alternatively. Manipulation attempts to persuade the subject to change their entire character with the utilization of distancing, distaste and, in the end, offering a feel better approach that fits the desired new personality. Hypnosis allows the subject to enter into another modified perspective in which they will be forced to be demanding and open to new thoughts.

On the other hand, manipulation will modify the subject's current point of view using subterfuge as an essential strategy, while influence includes the impact on an individual's convictions, state of mind, expectations, inspirations, or practices. With the exception of mental conditioning and deception, manipulation is a tool that can be used in a positive way to achieve objectives or goals. It all depends on the type of manipulation involved and the purpose of the person who needs to apply it. It also depends on whether the target or subject of the manipulation will benefit from it.

Many thanks to you for reading this wonderful piece. I really hope you liked it!! You are presently equipped with incredible methods that you can use from various perspectives. Use this information shrewdly and wisely.

www.ingramcontent.com/pod-product-compliance
Ingram Content Group UK Ltd.
Pitfield, Milton Keynes, MK11 3LW, UK
UKHW021335290825
7645UKWH00033B/380